THE LAND
STILL LIVES

THE LAND
STILL LIVES

JERRY APPS

FOREWORD BY
SENATOR GAYLORD NELSON

WISCONSIN HISTORICAL SOCIETY PRESS

Published by the Wisconsin Historical Society Press
Publishers since 1855

The Wisconsin Historical Society helps people connect to the past
by collecting, preserving, and sharing stories. Founded in 1846,
the Society is one of the nation's finest historical institutions.
Join the Wisconsin Historical Society: wisconsinhistory.org/membership

First edition published 1970 by Wisconsin House, Ltd.
Wisconsin Historical Society Press edition published 2019

Printed in Wisconsin, USA
Designed by Nancy Warnecke, Moonlit Ink

23 22 21 20 19   1 2 3 4 5

Library of Congress Cataloging-in-Publication Data
Names: Apps, Jerold W., 1934– author.
Title: The land still lives / Jerry Apps ; foreword by Senator Gaylord Nelson.
Description: Fiftieth anniversary edition. | Madison, WI: Wisconsin
Historical Society Press, 2019. |
First edition published 1970 by Wisconsin House, Ltd.
Identifiers: LCCN 2019009252| ISBN 9780870209062
(hardcover : alk. paper) | ISBN 9780870209079 (e-book)
Subjects: LCSH: Farm life—Wisconsin. | Country life—Wisconsin.
Classification: LCC S521.5.W6 A66 2019 | DDC 630.9775—dc23 LC record
available at https://lccn.loc.gov/2019009252

For Sue, Steve, and Jeff,
who one day will inherit Roshara

ACKNOWLEDGMENTS

I am indebted to Mrs. Charlotte Stewart and her brother, Weston Coombes, for relating to me their memories of Roshara.

My father and mother, Mr. and Mrs. Herman Apps, who well recall their childhood in the Chain O' Lake–Skunk's Hollow community, were the source of many facts related throughout this book.

Jennie Woodward of the Wild Rose Historical Society and her brother, Sherm Woodward, provided information about Wild Rose during the potato boom days of the early 1900s.

I hold a deep feeling in my heart for Floyd Jeffers, now deceased, who told me much about our Roshara and the people who lived there. I shall never forget his deep understanding of the outdoors and of the legacy of the land.

I must thank Howard Sanstadt, Barbara Vroman, and Arlene Buttles of the *Waushara Argus* staff, who constantly encouraged me in my writing about the outdoors.

My wife, Ruth, participated in every part of our Roshara adventure. She also read, reread, and helped correct the manuscript. I owe her heartfelt thanks.

And, finally, special thanks to Robert Gard for constant encouragement and creative suggestions.

CONTENTS

FOREWORD

Jerry Apps has written a story which, as he says, has no end. Its beginning is as old as the earth itself. It is a story of life—of the land and of one family that returned to it in search of a certain missing quality.

Apps is a man of ideas who is sensitive to the touch, the smells, and the feel of doing things by hand, today and a hundred years ago.

He talks of a purity and a simplicity of existence that, for most of us, is lost forever. The lush green hills and the lone-standing farms are disappearing under cities and ribbons of asphalt as we jostle together and every year find less room to breathe.

Perhaps we cannot return to the Apps cabin at Roshara, or to Thoreau's Walden, but we can affirm our own reverence for the land by doing something to protect it.

Today, the crisis of the environment is the biggest challenge facing mankind. To meet it will call for reshaping our values, to put quality on a par with quantity as a goal of American life.

It will require sweeping changes in our institutions, national standards for the goods we produce, a humanizing of our technology, and close attention to the problem of our expanding population.

Most of all, it will require that the people assert their right to a decent environment and that they evolve an ecological ethic of understanding and respect for the bonds between man and his planet.

Apps and his family have joined in an experience which ultimately must become the experience of us all. That is to realize that living is now, more than ever before, a matter of getting along with the environment in which we live, because our planet earth is the only known body capable of supporting life as we know it. If we ignore this fact, we diminish life for all living things and face the real possibility of our eventual destruction.

Senator Gaylord Nelson
1970

I

Prologue

The old black willow at the end of the windbreak is really six trees in one, but since two of the trunks have broken, only four fingers point skyward. The top of one broken trunk touches the ground, dead, smashed in a windstorm. The other trunk broke off three years ago and was removed. In the dead stub that remains, woodpeckers have pounded pencil-sized holes every few inches in search of insects living under the dead bark. From dead branches on the other trunks some of the bark has fallen off, exposing the furrows made by insects. To some, the old willow is shaggy and disheveled. Perhaps. But the shagginess gives the tree its character, makes it something more than other trees, makes it different from the ten-foot white pine that grows nearby with soft needles and organized placement of branches.

The old willow is surely not organized; branches shoot out from its trunks in all directions. Some are last spring's growth and olive green in color, some are several years old and already have furrowed bark, and some are dead with no bark at all.

A few years ago, lightning ripped away a strip of bark from the top to the ground, leaving a twisted wound in one trunk.

The end willow, as we call this magnificent old tree, grows at Roshara, our country farm in Waushara County, Wisconsin. The farm is one hundred miles north of Madison, where my family and I live, and five miles west of Wild Rose, our nearest village. Wautoma, the county seat, is ten miles to the south.

The community around Roshara is called Skunk's Hollow, no doubt for the many skunks denning there when the area was settled. The nearby community of Slab City is named for a local sawmill, long since closed down and moved.

The whole larger community, including Slab City and Skunk's Hollow, is called Chain O' Lake. It is the name originally given to the country school that, when it operated, lay a mile from Roshara. There are many small lakes and ponds in the region, and though they are not connected, the local folks think of them as a chain.

Roshara is an abandoned farm; no crops grown there now, no livestock. The farm buildings, once housing Guernsey cattle, pigs, and horses, are gone except for the granary we are making into a cabin and the old pump house that squats over the well.

The hundred acres of fields and woods rest quietly, but standing under the old end willow I can close my eyes and envision the corn and potatoes that once grew in the fields and the cattle that grazed in the pasture near the pond.

The remnants of farming days whet my imagination. Old fences remain partially standing, partially buried by grass, and they help me to picture the cattle in the fields. Four gnarled apple trees and several plum trees suggest an earlier orchard capable of keeping the families at Roshara supplied with fresh fruit.

Walking in the fields, I can still find cornstalks, not yet completely rotted, that remind me of the chancy corn crops planted by optimistic farmers year after year. And there are gullies, huge cuts in the hills, made when the rains washed down between the rows of potatoes and corn, ravaging the topsoil to the hollows. The gullies are inactive now, grown over with grass since the plowing stopped.

It's interesting to think of Roshara when it was a farm and to piece together what has happened to the land since it was homesteaded shortly after the Civil War.

Ruthie and I are interested in Roshara not as an economic venture but as a place to get reacquainted with the outdoors, to develop a relationship with nature and all its mystery and wonder. Having both grown up on farms in Wisconsin, we now want to offer the same experience to our three children, who at this writing are eight, seven, and six years old. Susan, the oldest, is blue eyed and bubbly. Steve, blondest of the three, is serious and interested in nature study. Jeff, the youngest, is short, husky, and interested in everything.

Our feelings toward Roshara and what it has to offer are deep and continuing. We feel there comes a time when every person asks, What is my life all about? Am I making it all it could be? Am I providing my children with opportunities that will help them seek quality in their lives?

We search out answers as we roam Roshara's hills, explore its wood lots, and walk by its pond. The questions prompt us to study Roshara's history and learn of its owners before us, people who got to know this land intimately and to love it.

Communing with the outdoors, on nature's terms, gives us a feeling of inward satisfaction and peace of mind. We seek to understand, to relate to present and past, to gain a feeling for the land. Our plan is not to change the land, not to convert it to some other man's image of what it should be.

We seek only to be a part of what is happening at Roshara. We do not wish to dominate. We search for solitude, freedom, and beauty, and with only enough environmen-

tal change to enable us to live there. We seek the opportunity to dream, to look at our lives and find meaning. Roshara is where we can do this.

II

Abandoned Farm

One cold winter day in the late 1950s the neighbors on the Wild Rose telephone line heard a general ring, five or six short rings that meant an emergency. Everyone should listen.

"The Coombeses' house is on fire!" the operator cried. Neighbors rushed to the farm, but it was too late. With flames leaping from the roof, there was no chance to save the old house. The pump house a short distance away also caught fire, and the neighbors managed to save it and the other outbuildings, but the Coombeses' home was gone. Clothing and furniture, what little they had, were lost. A pile of ashes, a twisted wood-burning cookstove, a misshapen Round Oak heater on its side in the cellar hole, these were left.

The willows in the windbreak closest to the house were singed, but they would recover. And the end willow, the one with six trunks growing as one, was far enough away to escape harm.

After the disaster, Mrs. Coombes and Weston moved to Wild Rose to live with Weston's sister, Charlotte. They never returned to live at Skunk's Hollow. Still, the fire had simply hastened the end of the Coombeses' farming days. They could not for much longer have competed with commercial agriculture or gained a living from ten cows on a hundred worn-out, sandy acres.

Except for a cornfield rented by Arnold Stea, a neighbor to the south, the farm lay abandoned, released from production. It could never, though, return to its natural state; corn, timothy, and potatoes had been sapping its natural fertility for eighty-five years.

In the first years, the weeds grew in profusion—ragweed, pigweed, lambsquarters. Without Weston's cultivator and hoe to cut off and bury them, the weeds grew undisturbed until the grass started returning.

Sown by the winds and birds, the grass crept from the fence rows where it grew for years unnoticed. The grass was waiting for the plow to quit the fields so it again could spread its soft green cover over the land. The grass roots penetrated the soil and tied the particles together, like a medication, healing the wounds cut into the hills by rain running over naked soil.

Slowly the soil's fertility improved, except for the most barren hills where grass would not grow. The old grass roots died and new ones formed, and as dead grass toppled and decayed, a dark-colored, fertile humus was left behind.

Rainfall determined how fast the grass cover developed, rapidly in years of heavy rainfall, much more slowly when slight. The green cover crowded out weeds, which could not compete with the dense grass whose roots soaked up all moisture and fertility.

With rainfall above average for several years, the wildflowers also returned to the fields. Unlike the weeds, the wildflowers competed with the grass, except in the more fertile valleys where the grass cover was most dense.

There was blue spiderwort; it could survive with little fertility. The sheep sorrel, with its small red flowers, and the hawkweed, with its erect, hairy stem and splash of bright orange, came back. The black-eyed Susan, yellow petaled with chocolate-drop centers, grew again, as did the tall and clublike common mullein, often called Indian tobacco.

After moving to town, Weston occasionally worked for my father, who lived a few miles north of the deserted Coombes farm.

"Anytime you want to walk around the old farm, Herman, go ahead," Weston said.

My father is tall, has a large but typical Apps nose, and wears glasses. All his life he has enjoyed walking in the outdoors, discovering new plants, learning the ways of wildlife.

So my father and I often walked over the deserted fields. There were entire hillsides of Queen Anne's lace, with leaves that taste and smell like its cousin the carrot when they are crushed and chewed. The delicate, flat-topped, white flowers gently waved in the soft summer breeze, contrasting with the orange and blues of the hawkweed and spiderwort.

We found sweet clover, both white and yellow, escaped from the hayfields of earlier years, gone wild and able to reproduce without help from people. Occasionally we found red clover. There was milkweed, with delicately structured and aromatic flowers that in late summer became seeds carried on the wind by God-made parachutes.

On the most barren hillsides where nothing else grew, there was moss. Entire hilltops were carpeted with moss, a soft place to rest and talk and think, a place to look out over the hills and see many wildflowers we couldn't name.

We walked along the rows of white pine trees. John Coombes, Weston's father, had planted them fifty years ago. The wind whispered through the soft needles. Stronger west winds had sent pine seeds into the field to the east and many took root. Pine trees were claiming the cornfield, changing it, never allowing it to rest.

Along the oak wood lot we noticed a similar occurrence. Little oaks were springing up, taking root in the worn-out soil, gathering sunlight into their leaves. This time it wasn't the wind. Squirrels had planted hundreds of acorns in the soft sand each fall, to be dug up for food in winter. But often they were forgotten. The acorns fattened with the spring rains and ruptured to send single stems above ground.

Sturdy little oaks they were, competing with the grass and wildflowers for fertility and light, and winning. Not in a hurry, these oaks. They had no concern for time, only survival, a chance to capture some sunlight and moisture and fertility each year and a hope that some hungry deer wouldn't bite them off.

We walked down the hill covered with blue vetch to the pond. The pond wasn't a quarter the size it had been twenty-five years ago. We talked about the marsh grass that was hip high where water had been six feet deep ten years ago. We noticed the popple trees, ever creeping from the woods and taking up space left when the water receded.

I'd asked, "How come? Why's the lake going down?" We both knew the lakes in Skunk's Hollow; they were water table lakes, going up and down as the level of the ground water rose and dropped.

Once the Coombes farm and all of this area was covered by a glacier that pushed down from the north and blanketed much of Wisconsin and the Midwest with ice. The huge ice wall pushed and scraped over the landscape, carrying along huge stones and soil on its journey south.

About ten thousand years ago the ice started melting

and retreating back north. The glacier left huge blocks of ice buried in the soil; when they melted, ponds and lakes remained. The Coombeses' pond was one of them, along with other ponds and lakes in the area.

But the pond was low now, lower than anyone could remember.

"Lots of reasons for it, I suppose," my father said. "Some of the old-timers claim these lakes cycle every seven years, seven years coming up and seven years going down."

"But it's so low now," I said. "How can it ever come back? How can it drown out all this grass and cover the popple trees?"

Father shook his head. I could tell he wondered too. "Can't help but believe that the irrigating on the prairie has something to do with it," he commented. "Those pumps often run night and day when the weather is dry. I can sit outside on a still night and hear the diesel engines roar as they pump water. Can't help but believe it's affecting the water table. Time will tell, I suppose."

He was referring to the level land a few miles to the west that in recent years had become a huge vegetable garden. Acres of green beans, cucumbers, and sweet corn were watered by irrigation pumps that drew water from the ground.

We walked among the buildings that remained on the farmstead. The barn, hip roofed and steel gray in color, had never been painted since its construction in 1912. Over the years windstorms had broken its back, tore loose its supporting braces so that the part below the roof line leaned south and the part above leaned north.

The barn didn't look safe. It appeared as if it could tip to the south and crush the granary or even fall right down and kill any animals tied inside. Still, the barn hadn't tipped in more than half a century; it just leaned a little more each year. As the old barn began to lean more, Weston moved the horses into the granary, where he made stalls. Either he overlooked the possibility of the barn's falling on the granary or he had no choice; the horses needed shelter.

We pulled open a squeaky barn door, went inside, and encountered cobwebs everywhere and the musty smell of old hay and cow bedding. Barn swallows nesting on the fly-specked ceiling joists flew in and out the broken windows. The cow stalls were still there, stanchions for ten cows and a couple of pens for calves. And there were the horse stalls—enough room for two horses.

Carefully we climbed the wooden ladder (one rung broken) to the hayloft. Could our weight tip the old barn? The hayfork, streaked with sparrow droppings, rested in the peak of the roof, its rope looped over a dusty supporting beam. Two or three feet of crumbly, choking timothy hay covered the floor.

———

Sometimes while exploring the Coombes farm, my father and I sat in the shade of the end willow to rest and talked about his boyhood in Skunk's Hollow. Having grown up on a farm just over the hill from the Coombes place, he remembered the huge flocks of mallards that flew over Skunk's Hollow and often landed on the ponds.

One day in late October his father suggested, "Why don't you and your brother go over to the pond tomorrow morning and see if the mallards are in?" The next morning before daylight, Fred, who was about fifteen then, and my father, nine or ten, headed for the little skiff they kept on the pond. A thin scrim of ice lay near the shore, and steam was rising from the water that hadn't yet frozen. Fred got in the front of the rather unsteady skiff and my father in the back.

The fog was so thick they couldn't see across the pond in the early light. Newly frozen ice tinkled like little bells as Fred slowly paddled the skiff out into open water. My father cradled the family's old ten-gauge double-barreled shotgun in his lap and searched his pocket for shells. Breaking open the gun and sliding a shell into each chamber, he was ready for mallards if indeed any were on the pond that foggy morning.

A trickle of cold water seeped through a hole in the

13

skiff's bottom and came up over the soles of their shoes. But neither my father nor Fred paid attention to that. The skiff always had leaked. Their eyes strained to make out the shapes of ducks floating on the far end of the pond where ducks usually landed and fed.

They both heard the sounds at the same time, sweet music! Not the loud sounds of drakes showing off for females, but the "cwuck cwuck" of ducks eating an early morning meal.

Fred stopped paddling, allowing the skiff to drift in the direction of the sound. Both tried to see what they knew was hidden by the heavy fog. Then they saw the shapes of mallards.

"Get ready," Fred whispered as the skiff drifted closer. My father pulled back both hammers of the double barrel, raised it to his shoulder, and pointed it in the direction of the feeding ducks. The gun roared and the next thing my father knew he was standing waist deep in icy water. A few feet away, Fred was spitting icy water and cussing my father between coughs. The kick of the old shotgun had flipped the skiff and tossed both of them into the water.

Father held tightly to the gun, and Fred, still with the paddle in his hand, made motions of wanting to hit my father with it. But then they saw the ducks lift from the pond, leaving behind the ten or twelve my father had killed, which they quickly retrieved before grabbing the skiff and wading to shore. Although cold and shivering when they got back to the house, they had ducks, the purpose for getting up before daylight.

We often talked about the Coombes family. They had little money; farming in Skunk's Hollow barely provided a living. John Coombes, the father, had his own way of agriculture; he never changed over the years, never bought a tractor, never planted improved varieties of corn. In 1946 John suffered a heart attack and two months later passed away, leaving his widow, Ina, and his son, Weston, to run the farm.

They tried to follow in John's footsteps, each year planting the crops and each year harvesting less. Ina and Weston never bought a tractor or became mechanized. For them the old way, John's way, was how to farm. Unable to keep up with the work, they sold their cows.

By today's standards their home was a shack. The walls had never been plastered. Old cardboard boxes had been torn apart and tacked to the two-by-four studs for warmth. On the cardboard wall in the living room was a sign that read, "An old friend is a true friend." The house had no brick chimney. A metal stovepipe went up through the roof, extending a few feet above the ridge line.

On below-zero days, Mrs. Coombes and Weston huddled near the Round Oak heater, stuffing it full of chunk wood. Each day Weston replenished the fuel supply, for the stove had a great appetite. The heater was red hot, as was the rusty stovepipe.

Ina and Weston enjoyed their farm life. And a simple life it was. Instead of a car, Weston drove a leather-topped buggy and a team of work horses to town for provisions and to the neighbors for visiting. Where else was there to go?

My father and I recalled our visits with Mrs. Coombes and Weston when I was a boy. Small and wrinkled, she always had a twinkle in her eye as she told early stories of Skunk's Hollow.

She remembered the Indians coming through the hollow each spring on their way to the trading post in Berlin, twenty-five miles to the east, where they traded hides, trapped the previous winter, for supplies. The younger children and the older women rode on travois tied to the sides of the horses. The Indians camped near the pond as they rested on their journey to the Fox River trading post. Their campfires sent spirals of oak smoke skyward, and Mrs. Coombes was often frightened. "But there was nothing to be scared of," she said. "We never had any trouble; we didn't bother them, they didn't trouble us."

From the closet she brought a pail heaped with Indian arrowheads, explaining, "John found these plowing the back forty near the lake." Some of the arrowheads were copper, corroded to a rich dark green. But most were of stone that was carefully shaped and chipped so the edges were sharp enough to penetrate the skin of a wild animal. There was a stone ax in the pail, the handle missing. Two grooves were carefully chipped into the sides of the stone and the bottom edge sharpened. The grooves were there to allow the stone to be fastened with rawhide to the handle.

Sometimes the conversations with my father were about central Wisconsin and how it might look in ten or fifteen years. I talked about the cities—Milwaukee, Madison—how crowded they were getting, with problems of air and water pollution, and wondered if pollution would come to central Wisconsin, which we had long loved for its clear blue lakes and streams and fresh, untainted air.

Dad mentioned city people who were buying land in the area, people from Madison, Racine, Milwaukee, Kenosha, and Chicago. How would these people change the area? Would they come to love Waushara County as we did?

Often my father and I discussed my children, who were growing up in Madison. They were yet babies; Sue was three, Steve two, and Jeff one. What opportunities would they have to explore hills like those in Skunk's Hollow, to look at the wildflowers and sit on the mossy carpet? In a few years they'd be old enough; already they enjoyed visiting parks and going camping. But what about five years from now? Would there be places for us to explore where we wouldn't compete with hundreds of others?

I told my father of my concern that the children develop a love for the outdoors, more than they could get out of a book or a conservation class in school. I wanted Sue and Steve and Jeff to appreciate nature through everyday experiences, to develop a deeper feeling for life. I wanted my children to learn how their lives related to the lives of plants and animals, to the soil and air.

My children and millions like them will, in a generation, make decisions about the outdoors. They'll decide about air and water pollution and the hundreds of other problems affecting environmental quality.

Will my children be prepared to make these decisions, I asked. Will they have the appreciation of nature, the knowledge and love for the outdoors that will help them in deciding about natural resources as a legacy for future generations.

I spoke of a recent newspaper article about people in an eastern city who had been asked what kind of street trees should be planted in their neighborhood. A majority answered, "We don't want trees on our streets; the concrete is much cleaner as it is. We don't want to rake leaves; we don't want filthy birds living in the trees and messing our sidewalks."

Father shook his head in disbelief. "How could anyone not want trees?" he asked.

Then I mentioned how nice it would be if we could own a farm like this old Coombes place, a place where on weekends and vacations the children could explore and feel and smell the outdoors as I had done as a child. I asked, "Do you think this old farm will ever be for sale?"

III

Our Place

"Place will never be sold as long as Mother's alive," Weston told my father. "She loves the old place too much to sell it."

Then one night, a year after I'd asked if the farm might be sold, Mrs. Coombes passed away. She'd lived eighty-eight years, most of them on the sand farm in Skunk's Hollow. When the farm was put up for sale to settle the estate, my father bought it, and two years later he deeded the place to my two brothers, Donald and Darrel, and me.

Now Ruthie and I had a farm where we could bring the children to explore, where they could run over the hills and fish in the pond, sit under the white pine windbreak and hear the wind as it rustled the long slender needles.

Ruthie and the children were excited when I told them. "Can we see it next weekend?" the children asked.

We left Madison at 5 p.m. the next Friday in heavy traffic. People were returning home from work; others were driving out of the city for weekend vacations as we were. The heat from the concrete streets permeated our automobile as we waited for red light after red light. The windows were rolled down and the stench of gas fumes hung in the car. The children were uneasy and too warm.

As we waited at a red light, Ruthie asked, "Why do so many people leave town every weekend?" The answer seemed easy. People wanted to leave the smells, the noise, and the congestion of the city. But were there other reasons too?

Finally we were past the airport, northbound on Highway 51, and the heavy traffic now moved more rapidly. As we stopped for gas near Interstate 90/94, the children counted the cars with camper trailers or boats. About every fifth car, we thought, was pulling some kind of recreational equipment.

People from Chicago and Milwaukee were going to northern Wisconsin for the weekend or for longer vacations. The cities were turning out their residents much as a school turns out its students in June. Many of the cars would return Sunday evening, but every Friday for the rest of the summer the cycle would be repeated.

Soon we were on Highway 22, and the traffic became lighter as we drove into Montello past the granite quarry and then on to Wautoma.

We turned right on the gravel road that goes by the farm, and Ruthie said, "Notice how much cooler it is here."

The trees along the narrow road shaded the road and filtered the hot rays of the summer sun.

A few weeks earlier we had driven along a similar country road and it too was shaded and cool. We saw songbirds, brown thrashers and bright yellow goldfinches. The boys glimpsed a cottontail that pushed its nose out of the underbrush, looked around, and then hopped back into the dense cover along the road. We noticed a herd of Holstein cows resting under tall oaks on both sides of the road. They were contentedly chewing cuds in the shade, waiting for the sun to drop toward the horizon and the temperature to cool before they would stir and graze again.

We met no cars on this gravel road, and Ruthie commented how quiet it was.

But today everything was different. What had been a peaceful country lane lined with oaks and overgrown with dogwood, wild grape, and hazel was now naked. Freshly graded ditches and a seemingly endless stretch of bare, newly graveled road greeted us.

"What have they done?" Ruthie asked in dismay.

Along the entire stretch of road, only three elms had been spared by the road crew's noisy chainsaws. There were piles of ashes along the roadside where the trees, some more than a hundred years old, had been piled like toothpicks, drenched with fuel oil, and burned.

There were no birds, no wild animals.

The newly graded road looked like a wide, brown line that a giant hand had drawn across the countryside. It was bare and drab. But, as new roads go, it was a fine example. It was probably half again as wide as the old road. And surely straighter. Now I could drive it at sixty miles an hour without easing my foot from the accelerator.

Later, I asked a man who lived near our place why the road had been graded. "It's because of the snow," he answered. "With all the brush the snow plugs up the road. Was so narrow the snowplow couldn't get through."

He told me the old road did need improvement; it was rough and often impassable when the frost left the ground in spring. "But to get state aids," he said, "the road must be a minimum number of feet wide."

My neighbor said he loved the trees and shrubs that grew along the road. He enjoyed the birds and wild animals that lived in the thick brush. And he sounded bitter about what had happened. "Some clever road engineer sitting in Madison must have figured the distance required for state aids so all the trees and shrubs would need to be rooted out to meet the requirement," he said.

"Oh, they offered to pay damages for the trees in front of my house. But how do you buy seventy-five years? It takes that long for an oak tree to reach shade size, you know. How do you buy time?" the man asked dejectedly.

The trees still grow along our own farm road, but for

how long? How could we save them when the road crews come with bulldozers and chainsaws intent on "improving" the road?

We turned off onto our own drive. Once our driveway had been a town road that ran through our entire farm, a full half-mile. It also went to another abandoned farm just west of our property, the old Stickles place.

Mrs. Coombes had once told us about the mailman with his buggy and team of sleek black horses. He had driven the road, past the Coombeses' house, down the long hill to the pond, past the pond, and up another hill to the Stickleses' mailbox. Heavy spring rains washed out the road each year as the water hurried to the pond. When the mailman switched to a Model T Ford in 1922 he found the going even more difficult, but by then the Stickleses had moved away and the mailman didn't have to travel the road anymore. The road has grown thick with grass and in many places with shrubs and large trees. We sort of go around these.

The old road made a good driveway and a good trail to the pond.

We stopped the car under the old end willow. The whole area seemed very quiet, especially to city dwellers. There was not the background rumble of traffic ever present in the city. The only sounds were the wrens singing in the willows and the gentle sough of the wind as it moved the narrow willow leaves. We heard a quail whistling "bob-white, bobwhite."

"What's that?" Steve asked.

I told him about the bobwhite, a brown quail with a white throat and a white stripe over its eyes, about the size of a meadowlark.

"When I was a boy, Steve, my brothers and I tried to whistle like bobwhites, tried to call them. One time we whistled a quail right up to our house," I said.

The smells were different too. Here on the old farm the smells were of life, of wildflowers, of green grass, of pine trees, of unpolluted air that washed our faces with its cleanness.

And there was room, space, distance. The children could run and play without danger from cars and trucks. Instead of row after row of homes, here were open fields and small wood lots, the pond, butterflies and crickets and grasshoppers and ants to intrigue the children.

As we watched the sunset, I realized other reasons that people left the city on weekends. Here in the country, on an abandoned farm, we could make some kind of sense out of our lives and break the hectic pace of a city life where everyone seems to hurry just to get someplace to wait. Here on the land we could fish and hike or just sit and soak up the solitude.

We could see the sun settle below the fields and woods

at the end of day, see the multicolors of sunset undistorted by neon lights and street signs that obscure our view in the city. Here we could find a break from city life, a change that everyone occasionally needs.

We walked around the leaning barn, past the granary and the pump house with its one wall charred. We peered into the cellar hole where the house once stood; the twisted and rusty stoves were still down there, other silent reminders of the fire that had driven Mrs. Coombes and Weston off the farm.

"Where we gonna sleep, Dad?" Jeff asked as he turned toward me with a serious look on his small round face.

IV

Once a Fine Barn

Sleeping at the farm would be a problem. The barn leaned more than I remembered. If it fell, the granary, with attached wagon shed and corncrib on one side and chicken coop on the other, would surely be crushed.

That left the pump house.

"You'll never get me to sleep in there," Ruthie said.

I didn't disagree. Sleeping in a well house didn't appeal much to me either, and besides, the structure was too small.

"Let's look at some of those build-it-yourself summer cabins," Ruthie suggested.

When we returned to Madison, we visited a local lumber company that sold do-it-yourself A-frame cabins. We liked the model erected in the parking lot.

The three basic sizes were twenty-four feet by twenty-four feet, twenty-four by thirty-two, and twenty-four by forty. According to the salesman we would get enough building material, precut, to complete the "uninsulated exterior" of the building. There were concrete piers and timbers for the base foundation. The A-frames were pre-assembled and ready to erect. And there was an upstairs, too, where the children could sleep. You could get extras, a front deck with benches, Shakertown shingles rather than those made of asphalt, a circular stairway to the loft.

We pictured the cabin sitting on the hill just above the pond, where we could look across the pond and see the thick oak and maple woods to the west and the open fields to the south and east.

The picture disintegrated in my mind when the salesman casually added, "You get all this for $3,000. Of course, extras like the front deck, the wood shingles, and the stairway will bring it up another $700. We'll deliver it, too, for about $100."

Nice as the cabin might be, all new and modern, we didn't have $3,800. And that was for just the shell, nothing on the inside. We would get a truckload of lumber, all pre-cut, true, but I have trouble repairing a leaky faucet. Building a cabin almost from scratch seemed monumental.

So we left the lumberyard. "Didja buy it?" Steve asked. "We gonna get the cabin?"

"Nope, not this year. We'll have to make do," I said.

The next weekend we visited Roshara again for another look. A place to sleep was on my mind as I again inspected the old leaning barn.

What a beautiful structure it was. According to all laws of gravity, it shouldn't have been standing, but the southern lean seemed to balance the northern lean and keep the building in a stable tension.

The matched fir boards ran horizontally rather than vertically as with most barns. The fir lumber had weathered to many shades of gray, darker around the knots and lighter where many rains had washed it. I pictured how the barn must have looked in 1912 when new. Then it was probably the finest barn in Skunk's Hollow, standing straight and smelling of new lumber.

How could we save it? Would it be worth the effort? Many of the original cedar shingles were now missing, battered by more than fifty years of wind and rain, sleet and snow. Huge shafts of sunlight pierced through the holes and splattered on the dusty hay in the loft, leaving circles of diffused light. On a sunny day to walk in the loft was to walk among columns of light made from dust particles reflecting the sun's rays. The roof leaked badly. There was a pile of rotting hay under each hole, and the boards of the floor were rotting as well.

Eventually, I thought, the weather will claim the old barn. The cancer of rotting wood may finally take her, or she will die in the fury of a raging thunderstorm and a gush of wind will smash her, twisted and broken, to the ground.

The barn was a home for birds and wild animals. In

winter rabbits ran through the crack of the partially open door and found shelter inside. Mice lived in the dusty hay. Swallows plastered their nests on the joists, hatching their broods of young each summer.

I had decided. The barn must be torn down before it fell and crushed the granary, and the granary looked worth saving. "Say, how do you tear down a barn?" I asked my friends in Madison. They answered, staring at me, "A what? Why do you want to tear down a barn?"

I asked an engineer, whom I thought should have the answer.

"Why don't you hire a wrecking company?" he said.

"But I want to tear the barn down myself."

"Better hire a wrecking company."

He knew the truth about my mechanical ability and mumbled something about wrecking a barn being dangerous, not a job for a professor of adult education.

For the same reason we didn't buy the A-frame cabin we didn't hire a wrecking company. Anyway, tearing down the barn seemed too much of a challenge to let pass.

It would be a shame for a wrecking company to come in with a crane and smash the old barn to splinters. We couldn't let the barn die that way. We'd tear it down ourselves.

Having never wrecked a barn before, or for that matter any building, I had questions: Do I start on the top and work down—construction in reverse—or do I start on the bottom and let the barn settle to the ground as I work?

And what about the lean? Whenever I cut down a tree it fell in the direction of the lean. How can I make the barn fall in the opposite direction?

The first decision was easy. I've never been fond of high places so no one was getting me on the rotten roof, particularly with the purpose of tearing it off. That meant starting on the bottom, but where, and how?

"Why don't you save the old boards, Jerry?" Ruthie suggested. "Maybe we can build a cabin with the lumber."

"Good idea," I said. What an accomplishment, to build a cabin from the wood of an old barn I had torn down with my own hands!

I borrowed a wrecking bar and a hammer from my father and began on Saturday morning. The half-century-old boards were smooth and gray on the weather side, filled with small cracks left as the hot sun dried the fibers and drove out the moisture. Near the roof, where the rain and sun couldn't strike the boards as easily, the boards were a darker gray, made so by a fungus growth that was easily rubbed off.

Starting on the inside, in the corner farthest away from the granary, I tapped the first board with the hammer; the nails pulled through, leaving two rusty holes. When I pounded the other end of the board it splintered;

the nails didn't pull through but cracked the dry board. The next board cracked, and the next. Only one out of five or six was salvaged, the rest ruined.

"What will Ruthie say?" I thought. "Our cabin's spoiled before we start it."

The dust stirred up by pounding the boards loose was almost unbearable. I removed two or three boards, then went outside into the fresh air to clean my lungs.

It was time to make more decisions. My experience that morning proved that little lumber could be saved for future building plans. And besides, destruction was taking so long. I worked half a day and didn't remove half the boards from the barn's north end. There were many times as many boards on the sides. "At this rate, I'll be five years tearing down this blamed barn," I said to myself.

I gave up trying to save the boards; it was no use. I tried to kick them loose from the still-sturdy two-by-four studs. Some would break easily; others wouldn't budge when I hit them with my heavy army boot. I pounded the stubborn ones with the wrecking bar and jarred them loose, but not before they broke into many pieces.

With disappointment I told Ruthie about my morning's activity. "It's going to take a long time, and I'm saving hardly any of the lumber," I said.

We were staying at my parents' place for the weekend, as we often did in the first years of owning the farm. "Tell you what I'll do," my father said. "I'll bring down the tractor this afternoon. Maybe we can pull the barn apart with that. You ought to get a burning permit too, so you can burn the splintered wood. Won't have such a mess then." From Miles Buelow, the fire marshal for our township, I picked up the burning permit.

The tractor speeded the process considerably. I hooked the chain around the boards and the tractor snapped them loose from the studs. We built a fire and threw the splintered wood into the leaping flames.

The burning dry wood crackled and snapped. If the barn had ever caught fire, all of the buildings would have burned. Just one small part of the barn, a few of the splintered boards, made a roaring fire.

That afternoon we tore most of the boards loose from the bottom portion. But we still hadn't settled a crucial question. How could we keep the barn from falling on the granary? "We'll have to think on that," Father said. "It's getting too late to worry about it tonight. Next time you come up we'll decide."

A few weeks later we were back at the barn. No change in its condition; the missing boards were not affecting its posture. "Think I've got it figured out," Father said. "We'll pull the studs out from the north side; then the barn'll have to lean to the north. Once we've got it leaning north and away from the granary, there'll be nothin' to tearin' it down."

I hooked the heavy logging chain to the two-by-four studs, one by one, and the tractor pulled them loose.

All that was holding the north end of the barn erect now was four, four-by-four-inch posts holding up a beam along the haymow floor. The area under the haymow was empty save for the posts; the board walls and the studs had been removed. The upper part of the barn seemed to be floating, but it was not moving despite considerable cracking and snapping as the upstairs support braces accepted heavier loads. The barn was refusing to surrender to two men and a tractor after its long struggle against the elements.

My brother Darrel and his wife, Marilyn, came by to watch.

"Well, what're you gonna do now?" Darrel asked. "You can't go back under the barn and hook a chain to those skinny posts. The old barn'll fall down any minute—just hanging there now."

"Can you think of another way to do it?" I asked.

"Nope."

I hooked the chain to the first post and quickly ran from under the barn. The Farmall tractor spun its tires a half-turn, and then the post snapped with a loud bang and slid out from under the barn. The barn stood as before, not moving a board. Carefully, I hooked the chain to the second post and quickly retreated to safety. Again the post snapped, but the barn stood fast. Now only two posts were holding up the north end.

I repeated with post three with similar results. Now the barn stood with but one skinny oak post holding all the weight!

"You can't go in there anymore," Marilyn said. "It'll come down any minute. See, it's swaying."

She was right, it was, and the snapping and cracking from the upstairs grew more intense.

"Let's just sit for a while and wait," Father suggested.

We sat for fifteen or twenty minutes watching the old barn in its death throes. It was a proud old structure, holding fast to its one thread of life, a skinny oak past. The barn wasn't going to fall until the post was pulled loose.

As I watched the old barn I thought of the cow stanchions I'd torn out earlier. They were rusty and covered with cobwebs, but they still operated. I pictured John Coombes's Guernsey cows standing in two rows in the barn, brown and white heads poking through the stanchions, eating timothy hay or cornstalks.

There were John and Ina, sitting under the cows, filling shiny pails with white foam-covered milk as the first rays of morning sun poured through the barn windows.

I could hear the baby calves blatting for the fresh milk, waiting impatiently for Ina to pour some of the warm liquid into a pail and thrust it under their muzzles.

I thought of Duke and Queenie, the work horses, pawing the stalls with their front feet as they waited for John to fork fresh timothy in front of them and dump oats in their grain box. For an instant I felt very sad, as though an era had ended.

"Guess that post'll hafta come out," Father said.

I stepped carefully under the barn, listening for a change in the sounds from upstairs. Underneath, the cracking and snapping from the protesting beams in the upstairs was much louder.

Cautiously I hooked the chain around the post and then hurried outside. I was covered with perspiration and my hands were shaking. I didn't want to see the old barn die. But it had to go.

"Pull it loose," I yelled to my father on the tractor.

The heavy tractor tires bit into the earth as the chain tightened and dug into the oak wood.

Then the post snapped loose and the north end of the barn fell to the ground in a great cloud of timothy hay dust.

One problem was solved. The barn would never fall on the granary. But it was a long way from being down. The south end was still erect, though now leaning to the north.

Later that afternoon Ruthie brought the children to watch us work on the barn. We were pulling apart the south end using the same technique we had used on the north end, now with the confidence of experience.

As the children watched, the south end crashed to the ground. When the dust settled, the children came over to look at "the strange barn with its roof on the ground." "What's that noise?" Steve asked.

"I don't hear anything," I answered.

"Don'tcha hear it, Dad?"

This time I did. Little birds peeping. With a rush of terrible guilt I realized we hadn't remembered to take the swallows from their nests before pulling down the south end. Now they were buried in the wreckage.

The swallow parents were circling overhead; they too could hear the cries of their babies buried in the pile of twisted and splintered wood.

"Get them out, Dad!" Steve cried, tears running down his cheeks.

I chopped through the boards for more than a half-hour, but with no success. I couldn't find the baby swallows, and after fifteen or twenty minutes we couldn't hear them anymore. Perhaps they had suffocated in the dusty hay from the mow. Or perhaps a board had come loose and crushed them. The barn was half down, but there was no happiness for the Apps family that night.

V

Exploring

The barn roof rested on the ground throughout the winter, buried under snow.

Early in March, with warmer weather, the snow slid off the roof and melted. Pussy willows pushed out fuzzy catkins on their slender stalks, a bright red cardinal whistled again from the top bough of the end willow, and the red-winged blackbirds returned to the marshy area near the pond.

In mid-March we too returned to Roshara and tore apart the barn roof, trying to save as many of the boards as we could. We saved the beams—beautifully grained oak four-by-fours and four-by-eights. And we salvaged the framing materials, two-by-eights and two-by-sixes. Full size, they had not been through a planing mill.

I marveled at the cedar shingles that had covered the roof for more than fifty years. The rains had worn the exposed part of the shingles to half their thickness; where they overlapped, the shingles were as they had been when new. I felt a deep appreciation for the stubborn wood, and when I held one of the old shingles in my hand it was, somehow, as though I held fifty years of sun and snow and rain and wind and summer heat. But my mood could not last.

Again we hooked the tractor to the rafters and jerked the roof apart. Trying to salvage the rafters proved an impossible task, so we dragged roof boards, rafters, and shingles onto the fire and burned them.

Now that the old barn was nearly destroyed, Ruthie and I again discussed where we could sleep at the farm. Waiting two or three years to save enough money for an A-frame cabin seemed too long.

"What about the granary?" Ruthie asked. "Any possibility of making a cabin out of it?"

"Not a chance," I answered. "Weston Coombes kept horses in there two or three winters. Doubt we'd ever get the horse smell out, and besides, it's not in very good shape."

"Let's have another look at it, measure it, and do some more thinking before we make up our minds," she suggested.

Ruthie helped with the yardstick. The main part of the granary was fourteen by twenty feet, the chicken house ten by fourteen.

"I think it's large enough," Ruthie said, "especially with

the upstairs that we could use for sleeping space, and maybe we could use the chicken house addition for a porch."

"But look at this wall," I said. I showed her where the horses had stood and how a hungry horse had eaten a two-by-four stud half through. There were holes where a hungry rodent had eaten its way into the building to get at the stored grain.

"And look at these windows," I said. "They're beyond repair." Almost all the glass in the three small windows was broken.

"And the door," I pointed out. "Just made of rough boards and warped so it doesn't fit anymore, can't even close it. The horse stalls have to be torn out, and that partition used for the grain bin, that'll have to be torn out. Look at that hole in the floor. What'll we do about that?" The floor had a large hole in the center where the concrete was broken.

"Come on, let's look upstairs before we make up our minds," Ruthie suggested.

It was a mess. There were cracked leather harnesses, scrap lumber, and a smother of dust and dirt. A small window in the west end had only two panes of glass, and there was a small door on the east end. We could see daylight through holes in the roof.

The stairway was a mishmash of old boards nailed helter-skelter to the studs; the first step was missing.

But the upstairs might have possibilities. The floor was matched lumber and sound. There was enough head space to use it as a bedroom.

I tried to picture the granary as our cabin. If cleaned, repaired, and remodeled, perhaps it could be made livable.

I compared the granary to the A-frame cabin and realized the A-frame, while new, would be only a shell, not too different from the granary. Once we cleaned the inside of the granary we'd at least have four walls and a roof.

"Ruthie, I think you're right," I said.

"About what?"

"About this granary. Maybe we could make a cabin out of it. Course it's hard to know what we've got until we clean out the inside."

"Okay," Ruthie said. "The kids and I'll start cleaning out the upstairs this afternoon while you're working on the barn."

We made many discoveries that afternoon in the upstairs of the granary.

We explored the two sets of stiff, broken harnesses, and there were parts of several others plus brass buckles and short lengths of loose brittle leather. One of three badly worn horse collars had been chewed by mice. Its straw insides were thrusting tiredly out.

Ruth and the children found four white oak bobsled runners, carefully cut and formed but lacking the iron shoes that should have been fitted to the bottom. Weston Coombes must have planned to make a new bobsled shortly before they moved from the farm.

There were slats from the reel of a grain binder—the part of the binder, I told the kids, that pushes the grain against the sickle so it is more easily cut.

The children found three coffee cans full of rusty nails. On wires tied across the rafters, John and Weston Coombes had dried their seed corn in fall and winter. In spring they shelled the grain from the cobs and planted when the earth was warm and ready. Thick dust covered everything in the granary. Four blackened faces appeared at the upstairs window when I asked Ruth and the kids how they were doing.

We quit work early that afternoon to put up birdhouses. In our basement workshop in Madison, the children and I had made six birdhouses from large coffee cans. I wired wooden tops to them and attached a length of wire so we could hang them from tree branches.

A raw spring wind stiffened our faces as we walked down the trail toward the pond in search of suitable places for the new tin birdhouses. Steve selected a clump of birch trees, and we wired his house to a lower branch. Farther down the trail we hung Jeff's in a black cherry tree. Sue hung her house in a willow tree near the pond, and Ruthie's was hung in a little aspen on the west side of the pond. Mommie had to have a birdhouse too.

My father had come along, and there was a house for him. "You kids decide where my house should be," he said.

We walked through the oak woods on the west side of the pond and up the steep hill that leads to an open field.

"Let's go farther," Sue suggested.

We walked along the edge of the old wire fence that one time kept the Coombeses' cattle confined to the field. Now the posts were down or leaning and the rusty barbed wire was on the ground, often covered by a thick mat of grass. We came to a little oak tree, about ten feet tall, that was growing alone near the fence.

"Here's a good place for your house, Grandpa," Sue said.

Grandpa wired the house in place.

"Bet I'll have a bird in my house before any of you," he said.

"Bet you won't," Jeff answered.

On our way back to the buildings we searched for branches to "grow" back in Madison. By putting the shoots in water we forced them to have flowers and leaves at least six weeks before they normally would. It was one small way to hasten spring.

We walked back to the wood lot near the pond. Here and there were sprigs of green moss, but no new growth. Everything was waiting for warmer temperatures and spring rains.

We found red osier dogwood, thorn apple, gray dogwood, black cherry, and wild apple. I cut a few branches from each. As we gathered branches we found ourselves in a blackberry patch.

"Ouch!" Jeff said. "Let's get outta here."

"How come there're picky bushes in our woods?" Sue asked.

"Makes a good place for the rabbits to hide; birds like the berries too."

"Let the rabbits hide some other place," Jeff said as I carried him out of the "picky bushes."

With arms full of branches we walked the trail up the hill to the granary. We saw little evidence of spring save for the patches of moss and green grass where the snow had melted on the south side of the hill. But we heard a robin sing as we neared the granary, and we knew spring was near.

A month later, in late April, we were again at the farm for a "planting weekend." The kids and I were going to plant a thousand small pines we had obtained from the state. The wrens had returned to the willow windbreak and the swallows were back, as well as the meadowlarks, the robins, and the bluebirds. And Jeff's birdhouse had a wren nest; the other birdhouses were unoccupied.

The grass was greening, and the buds on the oak trees were swelling, ready to pop open with pale green leaves in a few weeks.

The ice was gone from the pond, and the spring run-off had raised the pond's water level well above last spring. Killdeer were walking the shoreline. Tracks were punched into the bank on the west end of the pond where deer came to drink. A robin bathed undisturbed in the shallow water on the south shore, and a turtle stuck his head out of the water for air.

As we planted the foot-tall red pines, our task for the weekend, we enjoyed spring. Heavy rains had left the soil moist and our task easy. The plow slid easily into the sandy soil, and the slit stood waiting for the child with a tree to place it and stamp the hole shut.

We planted four rows around the outside of the farm and a few clumps on the open hillsides. We wanted our farm to be as natural an environment as possible, to change in its own way without help or hindrance from us.

The plow, turning the furrows for the trees, uncovered an acorn cache. We discovered hundreds, perhaps thousands of acorns. No doubt squirrels had planted them last fall, but why so many acorns in one place? Was the snow too deep for the squirrels to find their food supply? Or did something happen to the squirrels before they had a chance to uncover the acorns? We couldn't answer the questions as we planted pine trees through the acorn pile.

In an old gully we found a clump of box elder trees

that had been stripped of their bark to a height of two or three feet all around the trees. Their trunks were white, contrasting with the gray where the bark was attached. On the ground under the trees were chips of wood, a pile four to six inches high by each tree. We inspected closely and found tiny teeth marks on the debarked trees. Then we worked out the puzzle.

Field mice had lived under the snow in the gully through the winter and had eaten the inner bark of the trees. It was easy to guess the snow depth in the gully by the height of the bare areas on the trees.

We had other questions. How many mice did it take to eat that much bark? And why did the mice eat the bark this year and not in other years when there was deep snow? The trees were fifteen to twenty feet tall and would surely die now that their food-transporting vessels were eaten and destroyed.

Were there more mice than usual last winter? Were other food supplies for the mice exhausted? Was it impossible for the foxes to get to the mice and control them?

There were many unanswered questions as we planted trees and enjoyed spring.

An early spring storm had torn several branches off the willows in the windbreak. After the red pines were planted we sawed the downed branches into firewood length and corded them into piles.

The end willow had suffered most from the storm; strong winds had broken off several of its largest branches. One of the trunks lost its top. Now only five remained.

John Coombes planted the willow windbreak in 1912 to cut the frigid winds of winter that blew snow around the buildings and to take the brunt of summer storms before they pounded the farmstead.

From swamps in Springwater Township east of Wild Rose, John and Weston hauled black willows to their farm and planted them in rows west of the buildings. One tree was larger than the others, more sturdy and vigorous though it had grown under the same conditions as the rest.

"Let's put this big one on the end, closest to the drive-way," Weston suggested.

Several of the trees died that first dry August even though Weston, who was big and strong for his age, and his sister, Charlotte, carried many pails of water daily. But the end willow never wilted. It quickly adapted to the dry soil and grew rapidly. By fall the end willow was much taller than the others.

Several years later, when John was bringing in the last load of hay for the day with the high-wheeled wagon, he turned too short by the windbreak. Riding on top of the hay load, he couldn't see where the wheels were running.

In his haste to get the last load to the barn before dark, John drove the back wheel of the wagon over the end willow tree and broke it.

"Smashed the end willow," John said to Weston. "Musta turned too short at the corner. Shame too—it was the biggest tree in the windbreak."

The long slender green leaves wilted, then dried and dropped from the branches. The end willow was dead, or so it seemed.

But the tree wouldn't die. By the next spring six new shoots sprang from the stump and grew vigorously. Now six trees were growing as one, each competing but no single one winning.

VI

Tenting

It was dark when the last piece of willow wood was corded and the brush piled for some rabbit to find next winter. Soft city muscles ached from the physical labor as we drove back to Madison. During the next weeks many things evolved. We had a plan for the future, an idea in our minds for a home at the farm. But what about right now, this summer?

Where could we sleep?

We could sleep at Grandma and Grandpa Apps's farm while we worked on the granary, but that wouldn't be quite right, not complete and not in tune with our relationship to the land. We'd be missing something if we didn't live at Roshara and sleep there too.

"How about camping?" I suggested to Ruthie.

"Well, maybe," she said. She thought for a bit and continued, "But if we camp, where'll we get water? The pump doesn't work. And what about a bathroom? Bet you didn't even think about a bathroom. The tent isn't much good anymore either. Do you think we can live in it for two weeks?"

Mention of the old tent brought back memories. We had bought it the summer Ruthie and I were married and living in Green Bay. The ad we ran in the *Green Bay Press Gazette* said, "Wanted, used tent, preferably umbrella type," and our phone number.

The first day the ad ran, two parties with umbrella tents called. We ate supper early that evening and drove to the first address Ruthie had written on the telephone scratch pad.

A man in his early thirties answered the door. Yes, they had a tent for sale, and yes, we could see it if we came around to the back yard.

The man and his wife showed us their rather new-looking tent.

"It's been used only once," he said. "Bought it brand new from Sears last spring. Not a thing wrong with it either. Doesn't leak, ain't got any tears, got lots of room . . ."

"Why're you selling it, then?" I asked. The man looked at his wife, who had let him do the talking so far.

"I might as well tell them the truth, Joe." She turned toward me and said bitterly, "He'll never get me in that tent again. No more of this camping business for me. Slept on the floor of that tent, that's what we did. I was scared to death a snake or some wild animal would crawl in. Went camping just once—rained the whole damned weekend. How do you camp when it rains? No place to cook, nothing to do. Just the wretched sound of rain pounding on that flimsy canvas roof so you can't even sleep. It's awful, just awful. And that's why we're selling the tent. I don't want to see the damned thing again. I've had it with camping."

Ruthie looked at me, her eyes asking, "Is camping like this?" She had never camped before.

I had little camping experience to share with her either. My camping had been in an olive drab pup tent in a northern Virginia swamp. Our captain called it field maneuvers. The reason for camping in the swamp was to capture some imaginary enemy dug in ten miles from where we pitched our tents. "Camping time" was spent marching through the soggy swamp, looking for an enemy that didn't exist. Although we were in a swamp and often uncomfortable, I liked being outdoors and sleeping under the stars. But I hoped family camping would be more enjoyable than field maneuvers.

Hearing the woman's complaints, I wondered if there was a difference.

"How much you want for the tent?" I asked.

"It's $75," the man said. "And that's $25 less than I paid for it."

Earlier, Ruthie and I had decided $25 would be our top price.

"I'm afraid that's more than we can pay," I said. The man looked as if he wanted to keep the tent anyway, with the hope of changing his wife's mind about the outdoors.

As we walked to the car, Ruthie asked, with doubt, "About that tent, what the lady said, I mean. Is it true?"

"Is what true?"

"About the snakes?"

"What about the snakes?"

"You heard her. She said snakes would crawl into the tent, and wild animals too, and there were bugs, and you couldn't sleep when the rain pounded on the roof. You didn't tell me about the snakes and bugs, Jerry."

"Don't worry about snakes. They can't get into the tent. Most tents have canvas floors, and when you go to bed you zip up the door."

A tent was set up in the front yard of the second house on our list. At the front door a twelve-year-old boy met me.

"Your dad home?"

"Yup. Bet you're the guy lookin' for a tent."

"That's right."

A rugged-looking, middle-aged man appeared at the door, followed by another boy about ten and a little pig-tailed girl a couple of years younger.

"This guy wants to buy our tent," the boy said.

"Well, there she is. Crawl in and have a look. Pretty good shape for bein' ten years old."

It was a ten-by-twelve-foot umbrella tent with an extension in the back. One of the wooden poles holding up the extension was broken and fastened together with black friction tape, and a brass corner eyelet had torn out and was crudely sewn back in place. The tent looked serviceable, a bit faded but sound.

"Does it leak?" I asked as I tried to show that I knew something about buying a tent.

"Not a drop. Course it will if you touch the canvas when it's raining. Then it'll leak; something about breaking the surface tension that causes it. Keep your fingers off the roof when it's rainin' and you'll never have a speck of trouble."

"Why're you selling the tent?" Ruthie asked.

"Too small, it's just too small for us. The kids are growing up and we just don't fit. But we wanna keep campin'. It's been a big thing with our family—had the kids sleeping in this tent before they could walk. Hauled it all over the state too. Mostly stayed in state parks.

"Campin' sure has changed over the years; each year it gets harder to find a decent place to pitch a tent or park a trailer. Lots of people doin' it. Some of 'em I'd just as soon stayed home, the way they act; they bring along portable television sets and sit up all night drinking beer and watching the bloomin' tube.

"Those are the people who spoil it for the campers who are sort of . . . you might say, trying to get back to nature. Me and the wife both like to get our kids outta the city once in a while. Give 'em a chance to see the outdoors, sleep under the stars—how do you say it—get an appreciation for the wild creatures and the plants. Shame though, the way some people act, we're liable not to have many decent places to camp in a few years. But we're gonna keep at it. Can't stop campin' 'cause a few people aren't behavin' in the outdoors. So I made this travel trailer."

We'd noticed the trailer parked alongside the house when we drove into the yard.

"How much you askin' for the tent?"

"Kinda think it's worth $30, and I'll throw in this piece of canvas we used for a ground cloth."

The tent was old, the type with a center pole and an aluminum frame inside, not outside like the new ones.

"Course it needs a little fixing," I said. "Noticed that one corner had pulled out." I walked around the tent again.

"Tell you what I'll do," I said. "I'll give you $27.50 just as it stands provided you take it down and show me how to put it back up."

"Should be worth $30, but I'll take it. Come on, Jim, show them how to take the tent down and put it up again."

The older boy motioned me inside the tent and showed me how to take apart the framework and let down the center pole. Demonstrating how to pull out the stakes, he said, "Leave the corner stakes 'til last. Makes it a lot easier."

Then he showed me how to fold the tent in half, then half again, until it was a pile of canvas only three feet square and a few inches high.

I've always been glad that I bought that old tent. For seven years we've used it, camping all around Wisconsin. One year we camped our way to Manitoba, and the old tent served well. It has helped us raise our kids too. We started each child camping at a year old. In some camp sites diapers were a problem, but watching the children enjoy the pleasures of living and sleeping in a tent made up for the discomforts and extra work we had.

"If I solve the water problem and get you a bathroom, will you camp at the farm?" I asked Ruthie.

"I'll try it. I'm sure the kids won't care if it's a bit primitive."

There was lots of room at Roshara to pitch a tent, a hundred acres. We could select any site we wanted, not the site where some camp manager wanted to put us. We had an ice chest to keep milk and other perishables cool, and our gasoline lantern was a good light source.

"We'll haul water from Dad's place," I told Ruthie. "He's got some ten-gallon milk cans we can use."

The bathroom problem was still unsolved. The Coombeses' outhouse had survived the house fire and was still tucked under one of the willow trees in the windbreak. Branches almost completely hid the old building and blocked the entrance.

Like the old barn, the outhouse leaned—enough so the door wouldn't close—because the foundation was rotting, allowing the outhouse to slowly slip into the pit below.

The floor was rotting too. No one dared enter for fear of falling into the pit.

"Tell you what we can do, Ruthie. I'll see if we can get someone to build us a new outhouse."

"That's all right with me," she said, "as long as it's clean."

I asked my father if there were any good outhouse builders left in the neighborhood. "I'll do some checking," he said.

Not very many years ago everyone in Skunk's Hollow had an outhouse, but not today. Convenience has reached the country.

"Strange thing," my father said. "People used to go to the bathroom outside and cook inside. Now they go to the bathroom inside and cook outside, and we call it progress."

Next time we visited my father's place we asked about our outhouse.

"I called Jim Williams at the lumberyard in Wild Rose. He said he'd put a couple fellows on the project. They've made outhouses for the migrant worker camps, so they figured they could make one for you too. Jim said he'd deliver it out to your farm, but you'll have to set it up."

The children were excited when I told them we were getting a new outhouse; they called it a "potty house." I don't think they really understood much about outhouses, having always taken indoor plumbing for granted.

"When I was a boy," I said, "we only had an outdoor 'bathroom.'" I told them how cold that outhouse was in winter when the snow drifted through the crack in the broken window and piled up on the seat, sometimes covering the Sears catalog. But I don't think they really understood. An outhouse is difficult to describe. To know an outhouse you must experience it, and soon my three children would have the opportunity.

An outhouse is a distinct part of our farm's past. Tom Stewart, who homesteaded the land, had an outhouse behind his cabin, and the Coombeses' outhouse was still there, as I said, under the willow trees.

So our new structure is a link to the past, an opportunity for the children to experience what earlier children living on this land experienced. Our children, like the Stewart and Coombes children, would hear rain strike the small building, hear the soft sounds of willow branches brushing its roof.

Our children would know the feeling of walking the

path from the cabin to the outhouse on a dewy morning, when cobwebs sparkle with the first rays of morning sun and moisture drips from the outhouse roof. They might hear a mourning dove call and a wren chattering from its perch on a willow limb as they walk the outhouse path.

At night our children could walk the path and see bats swooping through the air catching insects; they'd hear an owl hoot in the deep oak woods near the pond. Slowly the children would come to know an outhouse and its tie to Roshara's past.

"When's the lumberyard gonna deliver our new bathroom?" I asked my father.

"Should be there by next Saturday. Isn't that when you're gonna start camping?"

It was the last week in July, vacation time. When we got to the farm with our camping equipment Saturday morning, the new outhouse was there. It was a modest structure constructed of outdoor plywood with a two-by-two frame and a red tar paper roof. It was a two-holer.

"I gotta go to the bathroom," Jeff said as he ran toward the new outhouse.

"Wait," I yelled after him. "Not yet, it isn't ready. We've got to install it."

"It looks ready to me," Jeff answered, but by now I was standing in front of the door.

At my parents' farm we found the milk cans and filled

them with water. My father volunteered to come back to the farm with us and help set up the new outhouse.

"Where you want to put it?" he asked. "It'd better be close. The thing's too heavy to move."

"How about over there, under that maple tree?" I pointed to the one growing in the willow windbreak.

I measured the bottom of the outhouse and pounded sticks in the ground to mark the corners of the hole. The rotting leaves, piled up under the trees each season, were scraped aside, and we shoveled the moist sandy soil to make the pit. In less than a half-hour the pit was five or more feet deep. Father and I dragged the outhouse over the pit and leveled it by tucking shingles from the old barn under the corners.

"There. Now you've got a bathroom. Never have to worry about the water pipes freezing either, although you might in the winter," Father said.

In Wild Rose I bought dark brown paint and enough shingles to start putting a new roof on the granary. Ruthie and the children agreed to paint the outhouse while I shingled. Each child was given a brush and assigned to paint one wall. Ruthie was in charge of the paint pail and general supervision.

Six-year-old Sue was the tallest and could reach the highest on her assigned side and thus paint more of it. Jeff, four years old and the shortest, couldn't reach as high so he concentrated on layering the paint wherever he could reach. It was kind of a mess, but it qualified as education.

From my vantage point on the roof of the granary I saw the outhouse slowly turn from a light tan to various shades of brown, depending on how much paint was applied, and where. Quite by accident Sue let her brush sneak across the boundary line and into Steve's assigned area. Steve, a little shorter than Sue, was already feeling slighted because he couldn't reach as high.

When Sue's brush came into his territory, Steve shoved a brush full of brown paint in her face.

All painting stopped as Ruthie declared a moratorium on hostilities and tried to stop Sue's tears and clean her face so she could see again. Normally Sue has blond eyelashes, but for that entire vacation they were brown.

"How do ya like it, Dad?" Jeff asked as I crawled down from the roof for supper. "Sure is a pretty potty house, don't you think?"

"Sure is, Jeff," I said, eyeing the camouflagelike look of the new outhouse. No enemy bomb would ever find it. But the kids had worked hard and were proud of it. I hoisted the boy to my shoulder and carried him over to the tent feeling pretty good about the whole thing.

VII

Summer Evening

Grandma and Grandpa Apps came to eat with us that warm summer evening, to enjoy chicken cooked on our outdoor grill, and sit in the shade of the willow windbreak and hear the children tell about painting the outhouse.

My mother, gray haired and in her middle sixties, had lived most of her life without indoor plumbing and couldn't understand why the children were so excited about an outhouse.

After supper I lit my pipe and shared with my father the problems I had roofing the old granary.

"That's one of the hottest jobs I've had in a long while," I said.

"Too blamed hot for roofing today, was ninety-two on our thermometer," Father said.

"It's sure nice being outdoors though. You know, roofing is one job where you can see progress. Each blow of the hammer gets you a little further. The results of your work are there for all to see."

Father leaned back in his chair and rubbed his bald head. "Sure not like that in lots of jobs these days. Never cared for a job where I couldn't see progress. Maybe that's the reason I liked farming; most of the time I could see some results. I could see the corn and oats come up in the spring, and after harvest the oat bin full and the corncrib running over with plump ears.

"I could see the little calves grow into heifers and then into cows. If you worked hard, yes, and used your head, you could see progress. If I had a bad year—well, next year might be better.

"I've always wanted to see where I've been. Gives me an idea of where I need to go. Lots of folks are sure confused about where they're going these days. Think part of it's because they can never see any progress, can't see where they've been. Do 'em some good to work on something once in awhile where they can see results, where they can show somebody else what they've done."

"I guess that's how I feel about the granary roof," I said. We sat in the shade, enjoying the early evening and the coolness. The children were playing in the old end willow. The thick green foliage filtered the hot rays of the late afternoon sun and provided a cool play area.

Sometime before I had tied the old hayfork rope from

a limb of the tree, and the children were swinging and yelling "Tarzan of the apes."

My cousin Duane, who had come along with my folks for supper, said, "Hey, you guys, you ought to be yelling 'Tarzan of the Apps.'" Duane, tall, thin, and in his early twenties, had recently returned from a year in Vietnam. Now he was relaxing, helping my parents with some summer work, but mostly trying to adjust again to civilian life.

"Let's walk down to the pond," I suggested.

We walked down the trail toward the pond, the youngsters, Grandpa Apps, Duane, and I. The grass on the hillside, so green and luxuriant in the early days of summer, was now tall, shaggy, and in places straw colored. The oaks and maples in the deep woods beyond the pond were dark green, not the many shades of lighter green so evident in spring.

The goldenrods were starting to bloom. The hawkweed's orange was a subtle contrast to the yellowish-green grass.

The pond was smooth and undisturbed except for an occasional water bug that kicked its way along the surface. Sometimes a whirlpool formed when a bluegill surfaced to grab a kicking bug for supper.

"What kinda fish are those?" Steve asked as he pointed at the edge of the water.

"They're bullheads, Steve. See those little horns sticking out just behind their heads? And see how big their heads are."

"They look ugly," Steve said.

Steve pulled the bushy head from a timothy spear and tossed it into the pond. A fish surfaced to have a look, and soon a half-dozen bluegills gathered around the floating timothy head, speculating whether it was food.

Jeff tossed in another timothy head, and from a deep part of the pond a large bluegill surfaced and grabbed the timothy head with one motion. Both timothy and bluegill disappeared. Either the bluegills were very hungry or they were looking for some variety in their diet.

A few seconds later the badly chewed timothy came to the surface and floated toward shore. No doubt one surprised and disappointed bluegill rested on the bottom of the pond, wondering what it was that had looked so good and tasted so terrible.

We saw a turtle swimming in the pond; it saw us and quickly submerged. In a few seconds the turtle rose to the surface again, only this time just the tip of its nose stuck out of the water.

"See this," Duane said as he chased something in the grass. He caught a garter snake about two feet long and held it up, holding tightly to its body just back of the head.

"Look out, it'll bite!" Sue cried excitedly. She and the boys scampered back a few steps.

"It won't hurt you," Duane said. "Come on and touch it. I'll hold it."

Jeff was the bravest. He shuffled close enough to have a good look, carefully stuck out a finger and touched the snake, then quickly pulled back.

"He feels nice," Jeff said.

If little Jeff was brave enough to touch a snake, then his older brother and sister had to do it too, or risk some teasing. Soon all three were touching the snake.

I told them garter snakes were quite harmless, that they eat mice and earthworms and frogs, and that garter snakes are as afraid of people as people are afraid of them. When a garter snake sees a person it'll crawl out of sight if it has a chance.

"Funny thing," I said. "People are often afraid of something that's different and they can't understand. And because a few snakes, like the rattlers and the copperheads, are poisonous, many people are afraid of all snakes. Roshara would be run over with mice if it weren't for foxes and owls and garter snakes to keep them in balance. It's all part of nature's plan to keep everything in balance."

The kids were impressed with the snake's tongue moving quickly in and out of its mouth, testing and probing.

"See, kids," Duane said. "His tongue won't hurt you. He's only trying to discover what's going on. He uses his tongue to do it."

Jeff stuck out his own tongue a couple of times, trying to mimic the snake. "Nothin' happens when I stick out my tongue. See? I'll do it again. I'm not discovering anything."

"You don't crawl around in the grass either, Jeff," Duane said. "You and the snake are quite different. You can feel things with your fingers; the snake doesn't have fingers so he uses his tongue."

Duane let the snake go, and we watched it slither away through the tall grass, toward the willow brush that grows along the south side of the pond.

Grandma, Grandpa, and Duane soon went home and we were left to the quiet of Roshara in early evening. A few wisps of horsetail clouds hung in the western sky, turning from cottony white to red then pink and lavender and finally black as the sun settled below the hills to the west of the pond.

The aspen, oak, and maple trees cast shadows in the pond and lengthened until they crossed the narrow span of water and finally disappeared as the sun sank away.

The wrens' chattering increased as evening approached. A swallow dipped low over the pond and captured a mosquito in midair. With darkness, the wrens settled down for the evening and in the distance an owl hooted.

On the hill above the pond a whippoorwill called, "Wheep poor WEEL, Wheep poor WEEL." This chunky, dark brown bird sings only at night and is seldom seen. In early evening it drifts like a shadow over the hills, gathering insects in short flights. Some farmers claim when the first whippoorwill calls in the spring it's time to plant corn, that the whippoorwill is calling, "Plant your corn, plant your corn."

A few seconds later another whippoorwill answered the first, and then they called together, "Wheep poor Wheep WEEL, poor WEEL." When we were back at the tent, a whippoorwill landed in a tree nearby, called once, but was apparently frightened by the lantern light and flew away.

In the semidarkness a bat zigzagged around the willow tree. I told the kids about its high-pitched call that bounced off objects and reflected back to tell the bat about direction, speed, distance, and location of mosquitoes and other flying insects. I told them that the bat will eat thousands of insects before daybreak, when it crawls into a dark place and waits for night again. "Bats are not so wonderful," Ruthie said. I fell silent as I remembered how terrified Ruthie was of bats. Some people react that way.

A cloud of vapor rose from the pond as the cool evening air met warm pond water. The vapor rose about twenty feet and hung suspended over the pond and the valley.

The smoke from our campfire rose to the tops of the trees, then bent sharply and formed a lazy layer trickling toward the southeast.

Just before total darkness settled over our camp site, Ruthie and I heard a loud snorting noise, repeated again and again. Across the open field about two hundred yards from the tent, we saw a large deer jumping. Every time it touched the ground it snorted. In the near darkness we couldn't tell whether the deer was a buck or a doe.

I walked quietly down the path toward the pond; in the dark every shadowy bush resembled the animal. Then one bush moved, and it was the deer. It stamped a front foot hard on the ground, then snorted again loudly, like a locomotive letting off excess steam. The deer snorted all the way to the deep woods to the north; then the snorting stopped.

Crickets were singing, rapidly rubbing their back legs together in song. Their tune would slow when cooler fall weather arrived and their back legs moved less quickly.

There were mosquitoes too, looking for exposed human skin. Occasionally a mosquito found a spot on my clothing and pushed its drill through cloth and into skin. Only the female mosquito bites, I am told, small consolation when there are thousands of blood-hungry females.

Stars dotted the sky, a panorama of white flickering light. An orange moon crept from the eastern horizon, and an owl hooted as we crawled into the tent to sleep. A mosquito net protected the tent; safely inside we only heard them buzzing.

I was back on the granary roof by 8 a.m. the next day and it was already eighty degrees. I stayed on the side away from the sun, but by noon it was ninety-five and too hot to do anything except sit in the shade or go swimming.

Of course the children chose swimming over sitting, and after a light lunch we drove to Silver Lake east of Wild Rose. A solid line of thunderclouds was building in the western sky as we swam, but we gave them little thought. Once back at the tent we noticed the clouds were much closer, and every few seconds we could hear the low rumbling of thunder.

"We'd better have sandwiches for supper," Ruthie suggested. "Something we can put together in a hurry. That storm is moving fast."

When we finished our brief supper of sandwiches and milk, the gray clouds were hurrying overhead, some moving faster than others. The thunder was almost continuous. Lightning flashes illuminated the nearly dark countryside—much too dark for 5:30 p.m.

We put the cooking gear under a tarp and anchored the corners with stones. I made certain the tent pegs were driven to their tops and the guy ropes holding fast. When the first drops of rain hit, we scurried into the tent to sit out the storm. From the tent we watched light turn to dark as the lightning cut across the sky. We imagined we heard each drop of rain as it struck the flimsy canvas and ran down the steeply pitched tent roof to the ground. We felt the ground shake as the thunder roared. We felt the full power of a thunderstorm, much better than sitting in a building. It all seemed very close and wonderful, and we were a little nervous, too. It was just us and the storm.

The tent shuddered a few times with the first gusts of wind, but then it settled down to accept the deluge of water.

At first the children were frightened. "Is the tent gonna blow away?"

"Will the lightning hit us?"

"Turn off the thunder, Dad—it hurts my ears."

"When's it gonna stop?"

As the storm continued—it did for nearly an hour—we talked about the rain pounding on the tent roof.

"When I was a boy," I said, "my brothers, father, and I would lie in the haymow of our barn and listen to the rain on the barn roof. It was a beautiful sound, restful and rhythmic. My dad told us how our sandy soil needed the water and that we should always be happy when it came."

As we lay in the tent the memories all came back to me, and I tried to share them.

"I'll bet the birdies are getting a drink," Sue said. "Rabbits, too," Jeff added.

As quickly as the storm started, it stopped. We crawled out of the tent to assess the damage. The cooking gear was still firmly covered and dry. The tent was in good shape, except for one problem that turned out to be major. When I had hurriedly checked the tent before the storm, I forgot to tuck the ground cloth under it. Water had run underneath and was now seeping up through the canvas floor, soaking it.

We were in trouble. We didn't sleep on cots but placed our sleeping bags directly on the ground, and there was no time left before bedtime to dry the tent floor.

The children weren't concerned about our dilemma. They were too busy watching a huge rainbow that completed a half-circle in the eastern sky. As they watched, a second rainbow appeared directly under the first.

"Say, Dad," Sue said quite seriously, "the boys and I wanna climb the rainbow. Take us over there where it starts." "Over there" to the children seemed only a few hundred yards away.

Ruthie and I were mulling over the sleeping problem. "Let's sleep in the granary," I suggested. "We'll spread the tarp on the floor."

The granary had not been swept. The horse stalls were still on one side, the old feed bin on the other.

"It's pretty dirty in there," Ruthie answered.

"Yes, but the tarp is clean, and the kids can sleep on it."

"Well, all right, there's nothing else we can do."

I spread out the tarp and on it laid the children's sleeping bags. We tucked them in and went back to propping up the tent to hasten the floor's drying. A little later I went back to the granary with my flashlight to check on the youngsters. They were all sound asleep.

I flashed the light around the dusty room, and the beam caught a movement. I pointed the light toward a hole in the granary wall and caught a deer mouse in the beam.

It was an attractive little mouse, big ears, bulging eyes, a reddish-brown coat with a whitish vest.

"Guess what?" I said when I walked back to the tent. "Looks like we'll be sharing the granary with some deer mice."

"Deer mice!" Ruthie said with a look of anguish on her face.

"Of course they're nothing like house mice. They won't bother you at all; in fact, they're kind of cute." Describing the mouse I'd seen, I told her deer mice were native, but not the gray house mice. The house mice, considered pests by most people, stowed away on the boats of the early settlers to this country and multiplied quickly. House mice give a bad reputation to all mice.

"I don't care if deer mice are native," Ruthie said. "I'm not going to share my bedroom with them no matter how cute they are. Mice and bats! Ugh!"

The granary was also filled with mosquitoes; I was more concerned about them than the mice. I thought again about the decision to sleep in the granary. Already the children had welts on their faces where mosquitoes had bitten them.

I wanted to stay in the granary that evening, to get acquainted with it and the creatures that lived there. But perhaps it was asking too much to expect the children to suffer the mosquito bites. I wanted the children to have a growing relationship with Roshara, a series of experiences that, at least in the beginning years when they are young, could be pleasant and cherished. A bad night with mosquitoes might do more harm than good and destroy some of the love for Roshara the children were developing.

"Let's sleep at my folks' tonight," I suggested.

VIII

Bullhead Fishing

It was drizzling the next morning, so wet I couldn't work on the granary roof.

"Just missed a tornado," my father said. "Touched down at Wisconsin Rapids." Rapids is about thirty-five miles west of our farm.

I didn't tell the children, but when I told Ruthie, we were both concerned and decided to buy a small transistor radio so we might be warned of bad weather. A tent isn't a safe place during a tornado.

Once my brother Darrel, his wife, and another couple were camping near Black River Falls, in western Wisconsin, when a windstorm hit their tent. Each person held onto a corner of the tent and barely managed to keep it in place. Several other tents in the campground were blown down; branches were down throughout the area but no one was injured.

Leaving the family at my parents', I went alone to the farm, planning to work on the inside of the granary. It was a dark, lazy morning. I stood in the doorway of the granary watching the light rain, not really interested in working on the dusty interior. Then I saw Floyd walking down the drive toward me.

Floyd Jeffers, a retired farmer, lived on a farm across the road from Roshara. In his seventies, bent over and thin but rugged faced, Floyd spent all his life caring for his sandy acres and enjoying the peace and solitude. He never married.

"What're you doin', Jerry?" he asked.

"Makin' a cabin outta this granary."

"Cabin, huh? Gonna be a lotta work, isn't it?"

"Sure is, but it'll be fun."

"Course you know Weston Coombes kept his horses in there two or three years. Horse manure has a heckuva smell—especially when it warms up. Hangs on too. Stays in the building."

"How do you get rid of the smell, Floyd?"

"Well, you can scrape the floor and the walls and douse it all with that stuff they kill germs with. Course some of that disinfectant stuff smells worse'n horse manure. Sure rained last night. You in the tent?"

"Yup."

Floyd didn't say anything, but I knew he was thinking that city people who sit out thunderstorms in tents were maybe short on the best kind of judgment.

"Glad you're fixin' up the old Coombes place. Been an eyesore. Hurts all the local folks to have these old buildings standin' here with no paint. And that old barn leaning like the next breeze'd blow it over. You and your family gonna live here?"

"Only on weekends and during vacations," I said.

"Remember when these buildings were built, fine buildings then, but old John Coombes never believed in usin' paint—maybe he just couldn't afford it. Buildings slipped downhill through the years. Little paint would've helped."

I told Floyd about the deer we'd seen and how it snorted and pounded its front feet on the ground.

"Probably had a fawn someplace and thought you were an enemy. She was testin' you, tryin' to see what you'd do, figure out if you meant any harm. Quite a few deer this summer, see 'em all the time. Good place for 'em around here with the ponds so close."

Noon was approaching and Floyd shuffled off, poking his crooked oak cane into crannies that intrigued him. He always carried the cane, not so much for support, but as an extension of his arm. He tapped the cane against a wooden barrel standing near the pump house.

"Know why this barrel's here?"

"Nope."

"Weston used it to catch rain water. See that board hangin' from the pump house roof? Well, the rain came off the roof, ran down the board, and into the barrel. Worked like an eaves trough."

Every time Floyd came over I learned something new about the farm.

The sun came out that afternoon. Ruthie and the children returned, and I crawled on the granary roof. I was nearly finished putting on the new shingles; if the rains held off another day, I'd be through.

The youngsters were playing in the end willow tree. There was a place for them to stand where the six trunks grew out of the main one. They were imagining Indians camping near the pond. Or maybe they were pretending they were the Coombes kids, playing in the tree after hoeing potatoes all day in the hot sun. How cool it was, shaded from the sun, a breeze rustling the willow leaves.

They could see to the pond, past imaginary cornfields and imaginary cattle grazing on the hillside. The old willow was ideal for lively imaginations.

"How'd you like to go fishing after supper?" I asked the children when I climbed down from the granary roof.

Jeff didn't answer. He was running toward the chicken house, where we stored the fishing poles. Soon he was back at the tent with his little yellow plastic fishing rod, a line dragging ten feet on the ground behind him.

"Jeff, you're all tangled," Sue told him.

"I'll take care of my pole, you get yours," he answered.

After supper we went back where the old barn had stood to look for worms. I turned the moist soil with the shovel.

"There's one," Jeff said, taking the worm in his chubby hand. It wiggled. "He tickles."

Sue wasn't as confident; she let the boys pick up the worms.

Grandpa Apps arrived for a visit and joined our fishing expedition. We followed the trail to the pond, and I unwrapped each of the children's fishing poles, tied on a hook, and fastened a shiny red and white bobber to each line. I threaded a worm on each hook.

Jeff's hook had barely settled into the water when the shiny bobber was dipping and making a wide circle in the water; then it disappeared completely.

Sue yelled, "Jeff, Jeff, you've got a bite!"

In the excitement Jeff didn't know what to do. The bobber skidded in one direction, then in the other, and then it disappeared again.

I helped him pull a wiggly bullhead from the water. "I catched the first fish, you guys," Jeff said.

Before I finished taking Jeff's fish from the hook, Steve had a bullhead on his line, and then Sue had one. As fast as we could, my father and I baited hooks and removed little bullheads. Before an hour passed the children yanked, dragged, and pulled forty-five bullheads from the water. The largest was about three inches long.

Many bullheads fell from the hook the instant they came from the water. Steve held his pole in one hand and my trout landing net in the other. When a bullhead fell from his hook, landed on the bank, and tumbled toward the water, Steve clamped his net over the fish.

Then a frog jumped in front of Steve, and he decided frog catching was a more magnificent challenge than catching bullheads. He left his pole with bobber bobbing and ran hollering along the shore, trying to drop his net over the evasive green hopper.

Finally, after three or four near misses, he was successful. "Look, I got me a frog," he said. It was quite an achievement for a boy who had never before caught one.

Willows skirted the pond on the south. As we fished, a Baltimore oriole made flight after flight to its nest hanging from a branch in one of the tallest trees. The oriole's dark orange and black color was a vivid contrast against the dark green of the willow leaves. Barn swallows flew low over the water on the west end of the pond, dipping down to capture water insects.

A small birch tree near the pond had much of its bark skinned off; a buck deer had used the tree to rub velvet from his antlers.

Our fishing trip was a great success from the children's point of view. Catching fish, any kind of fish, no matter what size, makes the fisherman happy.

The next day the granary roof was completed, including a new roof over the wagon shed, corncrib, and chicken house additions to the granary. Next we could start on the inside.

There were many questions. How would we get rid of the horse smell? Would we need to replace the siding? In many places there were large holes where mice and other animals could easily go in and out.

What about the floor? Besides being cracked in many places, in the center it had a hole two feet across where the concrete had broken and completely disintegrated. What about the doors and windows? Those already there surely wouldn't do. What changes could we make upstairs?

When our vacation was finished, we packed up our tent and camping equipment and drove back to Madison. Our family experience, I felt, had been glorious in a simple and almost inexpressible way. We had done nothing really dramatic. Yet all of us felt a great excitement, as though we had a tiny helping hand in bringing something back to life.

The old farmland, worn out but desperately beautiful to us all, was in our hearts. Our children might forget the smells, the freshness of the mornings, but somehow the appeal of Roshara and the mystery of land and people would be with them always. I put my hand across the car seat and touched Ruthie, and we both knew that our quiet adventure was real and worthwhile.

IX

Roshara

"You know what our farm needs?" Ruthie asked after we had tucked the children in bed one evening and some sort of temporary quiet had settled over our Madison home.

"What's that?" I replied.

"It needs a name. We can't go on calling it 'the farm' or 'our-Town-of-Rose farm.' It needs a name that will give people a feel for the place, a name that hints of the rolling hills, the two small wooded areas, the pond in the valley with a clump of willow trees on the south end of it. A name that suggests wrens living in that old end willow near the cabin, and the bluebirds that nest in the fence posts on the far west end of the property. Jerry, we need a name that suggests red pine trees poking through the grass where we planted them."

"Be hard to pick such a name," I said, "but if we could I'd want the name to remind me of the past, when the early settlers came to this part of Wisconsin and broke the soil with oxen and planted the first crops to grow on the rolling sandy hills. I want to remember Tom Stewart, who homesteaded our farm, and the other farmers who lived on this land."

"Guess I never knew much about Tom Stewart," Ruthie said.

"Well, he was quite a guy."

On March 21, 1864, Congress passed a law making homestead lands available as a bonus to Civil War veterans with at least two years' service. The only requirement was that the veteran live on the property for one year and improve it.

Thomas Stewart, a farm boy in Rose, Wayne County, New York, responded to Abe Lincoln's call for volunteers. When he heard of the lands in central Wisconsin available to him as a veteran, Tom recognized an opportunity to discover a new life and to fulfill his long-time wish for some land he could call his own. In 1867 he came to Rose Township, Waushara County, Wisconsin.

Tom, who was six feet tall, had broad shoulders, and wore a full mustache, stopped at the land office in Wausau. At that time Wausau was a small but busy pioneer town in north-central Wisconsin, a trading center for the many settlers who were swarming to Wisconsin in search of new land. It had sawmills where white pine logs were sawed into boards—the best building material known—and general stores where farm implements might be purchased.

"Anything available in Waushara County?" Tom asked the land agent. "Like to settle in Rose Township. Friends of mine went there a few years ago."

"Well, let's check the list," the land agent said, paging the record. He thumbed the thick book for a few minutes, then looked up and smiled.

"Here's the farm you want. A quarter-section in the southwest corner of Rose Township."

Tom was pleased. Here was the land he wanted and it was near his friends. There were the Jeffers, the Jenkses, the Baileys, the Pageses, the Wileys, and the Wheelers, who had all come to Wisconsin from New York since 1850.

They named the township Rose, after Rose, New York. In 1874 the village was organized and named Wild Rose to avoid confusion with the township. The many wild roses growing in the vicinity made the village name romantically appropriate.

After building a cabin near the wagon trail that rutted past the quarter-section, Tom started right in clearing land that first spring. With his team of oxen, he pulled out the smaller oak trees, first shoveling around each tree until the tangled mass of roots was exposed. Then he hooked a heavy logging chain around each trunk and yelled "gee-ho" to the oxen. Slowly the chain tightened as the oxen pushed into their yokes. The oak roots cracked as the animals strained and then the stunted oak tree slowly tipped over and was pulled from the sandy soil.

When several trees were dug out they were dragged into huge piles and set ablaze. The smoke from Tom Stewart's fires could be seen for miles around, but no one was concerned. Everyone was burning brush and trees. Many farmers were clearing land they had recently home-steaded.

When a patch of ground was cleared, Tom hired Ike Woodward and William Henry Jenks to break the soil. Woodward and Jenks had a business of going from farm to farm with their breaking plow and oxen to open new land for $1.50 an acre. Partners in the business, each owned two yoke of oxen, and together they owned the breaking plow.

The massive breaking plow had a two-foot-thick white oak beam eighteen feet long, strong enough to ab-sorb the shock of the plow hitting stones and tree roots. The plow's moldboard was five feet long and cut a furrow twenty inches wide and eight or nine inches deep through the virgin soil. The moldboard was constructed to turn over soil never before disturbed. A short moldboard plow, the type used once the land was broken, wouldn't turn new land. With a regular plow, sod fell back in place as if it had not been plowed.

A pair of handles stuck out behind the huge plow and

were held by the plowman, who walked behind. The plow was sturdy. So was the plowman. Settlers claimed it took a good man to follow a breaking plow all day as it struck rocks and hit hidden roots. Woodward and Jenks were sturdy men, and they took turns holding the plow day after day, from early spring until freeze-up, as they broke new land on farms all over Rose Township.

It took ten oxen to pull the plow. When they came to the Stewart homestead, Jenks and Woodward hooked their oxen to the plow and added Tom Stewart's too. The plow turned the heavy sod, leaving golden-brown soil ready for the harrow and drag, and finally for the potato or corn planter. The fresh smell of newly broken soil hinted at the untapped productivity and suggested farm crops that would grow where once there was prairie and scrub oak.

Tom Stewart cleared enough land that first year to make a living from his crops. Two years later, on August 28, 1869, he married Maria Jenks. Now Tom had someone to help him in the fields, to prepare his meals, to share his disappointments and fortunes.

Satisfied with the improvements Tom had made on the land, the government granted him clear title in 1874. His wish had come true. The farm was his. He could have obtained title sooner, but the sixty miles to the land office in Wausau was too far to travel often.

In 1877 Tom Stewart sold his farm and moved to another south of Wild Rose. Then followed a long succession of new owners who worked the farm a few years and sold it. Joseph and Laura Hursh bought a hundred acres of the farm, and B. E. Darling bought sixty.

In 1886 Joseph and Laura sold the farm to William Hursh, who in 1900 sold it to George P. Walker. In 1904 Walker sold it to T. H. Patterson, and in 1908 Patterson sold it to D. R. Bowen.

By 1908 many farmers lived in the Skunk's Hollow–Chain O' Lake community—Ed Stickles, George Apps, the Jefferses across the road from the Bowens, and John R. Jones two miles north. Renting the Jones quarter-section was the Coombes family, John, Ina, and their two children, Weston and Charlotte.

When Dave Bowen put the farm up for sale in 1910, John and Ina Coombes bought it. Ina had always wanted to return to the old Stewart place, for she was Tom Stewart's daughter, born on the farm in 1876. Now she was moving back home. John, tall, soft spoken, and deliberate, had come to this country from England. They had rented many farms in the neighborhood but never owned one.

"I'll never move from here 'til I die," said Ina when they moved to the old Stewart place. Ina was small and thin. "I've made my last move. Now Charlotte can get back her health."

Charlotte hadn't been well. At eighteen months, she

had had a fever for more than two weeks when family friends from Wild Rose came to visit. Little Charlotte was thin, her face flushed and haggard. Her eyes sunken and glassy, she lay in her crib not moving, scarcely breathing.

When the friends returned to the village they said, "The Coombes baby is dead." No child could live with such a high fever, they reasoned. Surely Charlotte would be dead by the time they got back to town.

But a miracle happened—with some help from Grandpa Stewart, who put brandy in the baby's mouth and wiggled her tongue so she'd swallow it, and a pioneer doctor from Wautoma.

"Kill me three cats and four chickens," said the doctor. "Cut open the cats' bellies but leave in the innards. Do the same with the chickens."

The doctor covered the baby with the dead animals. "It was an awful sight," Mrs. Coombes said. "Blood dripping from the carcasses, running over the baby and soaking the bed clothes. The stench was almost unbearable."

"The animals' heat might save the baby. It's our only hope," the doctor said.

Grandpa Stewart hadn't changed clothes for two weeks, having been with the baby day and night. A neighbor said, "Tom, you're all in. You'd better get on home and get some rest or we'll be watching over you next."

"I'm gonna stay until three o'clock, then I'll go home."

Grandpa Stewart had a feeling that if the baby didn't show improvement by midafternoon she would die.

At three o'clock Charlotte wiggled a finger, the first sign of life she had shown for several days. The crisis was past.

Mrs. Coombes's Aunt Jennie never forgave them for allowing the family to give the child brandy. A strict member of the Woman's Christian Temperance Union, she said, "Why didn't you let the child die in peace?"

Besides remembering the people who lived on the land, I wanted the farm name to remind us of the wild rose flowers that grow here. Before this land was plowed there were entire hillsides of wild roses, soft and pink with bright yellow centers.

Wherever a patch of wild roses grew, the entire area was filled with their delicate perfume. Wild roses are quite different from garden roses. They open flat because their petals are not held together as with garden varieties. They're armed with sharp thorns too, protection from the wild animals that would try to eat them.

Now we've only a few wild roses left; they cluster along the fence rows where the plow can't get to them.

"Did you know wild roses were in the same family as apples and plums, Ruthie?" I asked.

"No, I didn't."

"Well, once the petals fall, the fruit forms—it's called a rose hip and is rich in vitamin C. Pioneers collected the hips by the pailful, cooked them up with water and sugar, and made rose jelly. Some people made soft and very fragrant pillows of the petals."

I had a thought. "Somehow the name we select must remind us of the wild roses. Got any ideas for a name?"

"Not really," Ruthie answered. "All I can come up with are names like 'Appses' Acres,' and 'Aching Acres.' Somehow they don't quite fit, although the last one seemed appropriate the day we finished planting red pines."

Then I thought of asking the people who read my weekly column in the *Waushara Argus* to help with the naming. I had written the column Outdoor Notebook for some time, and since acquiring the farm, our activities had often served as column topics. The readers already were familiar with the old deserted land and our love of it.

"Sounds like a good idea," Ruthie said. "Why don't you make a contest of it? Offer a prize to the person who suggests the name we select."

In my next column I asked Outdoor Notebook readers to suggest names for the old Coombes place, which we Appses now owned. The *Waushara Argus* has more than twenty thousand readers; I hoped for some action.

I wrote: "Our farm needs a name and I need your

help. We require a name that will give people a feel for the area, that says something of the farm's past. I'll present a bird guidebook to the reader who suggests the name we decide to use."

I mentioned that Bill Stokes, who then wrote an outdoor column for the *Wisconsin State Journal* in Madison, had a farm in Marquette County he called "The Back Forty." I said that Mel Ellis, novelist and writer of an outdoor column for the *Milwaukee Journal,* named his place "Little Lakes."

Less than two weeks after the appeal was published, we had received thirty-five names, and the cards and letters were still coming. They came from as far away as Lexington, Kentucky, and Indianapolis, Indiana. Lillian Polivka of Brookfield, Illinois, suggested fourteen different names on fourteen separate postcards received on fourteen consecutive days.

When the deadline arrived, we had forty-nine names and the problem of which one to select.

We went through Nature's Nook, Rolling Meadows, Willow Farm, Laurel Hill, Rosalie, Pineview, Bit of Heaven, Green Briar, Nature's Haven, Appses' Rose Dale, Sleepy Hollow Farm, Wildwood Haven, Lupine Lodge, Rural Rose Retreat, and Shady Nook.

We also considered Idyllwood Valley Farm, Dunbar, Buena Vista, Whispering Willows, Shady Willow Farm, Happy Hours, Yours and Ours, and Years and Ours.

They were good names, but which one said what we so deeply felt?

Two clever names were received from Ilda Rumquist of Indianapolis: Sha-Po-Pi-Ac, and Su-Po-Pi-Ac. The first name is a shortened Shady-Poplar-Pine-Acres, or if we preferred the sun to the shade, Sunny-Poplar-Pine-Acres. The first letter of each segment is *Apps* spelled backward.

Finally we were down to two names: "Innisfree," suggested by Nedra Buelow of Wild Rose, and "Roshara," offered by Ruth Pochmann of Coloma.

The name "Innisfree" comes from William Butler Yeats's poem "The Lake Isle of Innisfree," in which he tells of the peace at his secluded place and the small cabin that he was building there. We liked the sound of the name and the thoughts Yeats expressed.

But "Roshara" combined the township Rose, where the farm is located, and Waushara, the county.

We liked the musical sound of "Roshara," the ease with which it could be pronounced, its poetic character. But beyond the name's more superficial qualities we liked its deeper significance.

"Roshara" reminded us of wild roses growing along the fence row above the pond, the sweet fragrance inviting honey bees to drink the nectar.

When we hear the name we think of Rose, New York, and those settlers who came to Waushara County shortly before the Civil War and named the township Rose and the nearby village Wild Rose.

And we are reminded of Waushara, the county named for the Ho-Chunk Indian chief whom white people called "Big Fox." *Waushara* in the Ho-Chunk language means "foxes."

"Roshara" was right. It fit. It spoke something of what we felt for the land of which, perhaps, we were simply another part of its cycle.

X

The Seasons Change

The October after our first vacation at the farm, we drove back to Roshara to soak up the last days of fall before the snow came.

I stopped the car by the old wire gate we had put up to discourage intruders from driving to the pond. I'd made the gate from woven wire John Coombes had used to fence in his pigs.

One end of the rusty wire was nailed to a red cedar post, which John had firmly planted in the sandy soil thirty years before. Red cedar posts have been known to remain in the ground for many years before they rot and tip over. The other end of the woven wire I fastened to a six-foot birch post, cut from the birch clump along the trail to the pond. It made an admirable gate, and I could latch it by stretching the wire from the birch post end. A hank of baling wire attached the birch to a gate post. The invention wasn't mine, but it worked well for a "city farmer."

The grass, brown and tangled, was wet with dew, a dew so heavy it dripped from the wooden shingles on the pump house and dripped off the granary roof. Before long the ground would be covered with frost each morning.

An autumn haze hung over the pond, filtering the sunlight as it probed earthward. We walked by the white birch clump, its yellow leaves outlined against a cool blue sky. We inhaled the crisp fall air.

The maples on the far hill, no longer hidden in a forest of green oaks, had turned a brilliant red and orange and yellow. We easily picked out the maples from the oaks as more intense in color. In summer the oak leaves were a rich dark green on their upper surfaces, yellowish green beneath. But now they were various shades of reddish brown.

Soon the maple leaves would fall, as would the leaves of the birch and popple. The oak leaves would remain on their branches, dry and earthy brown, to rattle in the winter winds; they could hide a squirrel lying flat on an oak limb.

The pond was smooth and clear as we walked along its edge. In the damp sand were tracks of both deer and raccoon. A rabbit bounded from beneath an old brush pile, and we spotted a squirrel burying acorns. No one had to remind Mister Squirrel that it was fall.

On our way back up the hill from the pond, we saw fall in the brilliant red torches that graced the tops of the scraggly sumacs. The hazelnuts were ripe and ready for picking and eating, we thought at first, but close inspection revealed in each nut neat holes made by worms dining on the meat so that only shells remained.

A few wildflower stragglers lingered to accentuate the landscape with splashes of ground-level color. The goldenrods, some still yellow, were now often shaggy and a fluffy white.

The wild apple trees at Roshara (several remain from random wild plantings years ago) had released their annual crop of bright red fruit, encouraged by fall rains and wind. Only a few apples stuck fast to the branches, soon to be bare. The dying grass under the trees had been smashed down by deer foraging the sour wild apples.

Greenish-white berries, like miniature Christmas tree ornaments, clung to the branches of the gray dogwood, sustenance for the birds who chose to winter at Roshara.

Ample rains of summer had produced a bountiful crop of wild grapes, some hanging from vines that wound halfway to the top of the oak trees.

The last remnants of the blackberry crop hung where the frost had not yet touched. But the dark berries were scarce. Birds had plucked nearly all from their barbed canes. Head high, the blackberry canes waited to tear at the fur of any deer that chose to go through rather than around the clump.

And the brambles waited to tear at the frail skin of the deer hunter who, in the heat of the chase, stumbled into the tangle, not realizing until too late that he would emerge with many scratches on legs and arms.

We stopped to listen for the honking of wild geese angling south from Canada but heard nothing. We watched a pair of mallards through the trees, circling, getting ready to set down on the pond, a place to rest and feed before they moved on again.

I remembered the stories Mrs. Coombes had told of earlier days when flock after flock of Canada geese wended their way south. Lines of geese darkened the sky from one horizon to the other, she said, their calls telling of fall and the winter season to follow. Some flocks had hundreds of geese, flying together in a long-tailed "V." Other groups had many fewer and spaced themselves in staggered formations, each one a little different from the others.

Occasionally a flock lighted on the pond to rest for the night. The hungry migrants visited the nearby cornfield, searching for corn kernels, gaining new strength for their flight the next day.

Mrs. Coombes named the ducks flying south: blue-winged teal, canvasbacks, wood ducks, and mallards—always more mallards than the other kinds, shiny green-headed drakes with white collars, brown breasts, and gray bodies, accompanied by the dull brown females. The ducks also stopped at the pond to rest, eat, and spend the night before continuing their journey. Often when these visitors from the north lifted from the pond they were joined by other mallards that had hatched and grown up on the farm.

She said Weston had watched two mallard families all one summer, from the time the females built nests until the young ducklings were grown. One pair of ducks nested on top of a deserted muskrat house that emerged a few feet above the surface of the pond. The nest was dry, yet water surrounded it. Many of these home-grown mallards returned again the next spring, Mrs. Coombes said, seeking nesting sites on the pond. Others journeyed on farther north.

There was still work to be done at Roshara before winter had its place on the stage of the drama of seasons. The pump needed draining. A small valve in the well pit could drain water from the pipe that stuck above ground and keep the system from freezing and breaking. At one time a heavy wire was attached to the valve so you could manipulate it without crawling into the pit. But long before we acquired the farm the wire was broken. Crawling into the well pit wasn't an especially pleasing task.

John or Weston Coombes had constructed a ladder from two unsawed pieces of oak wood with some smaller oak branches nailed across for steps. Only two steps remained, one near the top and the other about halfway to the bottom of the six-foot hole.

Steve and Jeff helped me nail together a new ladder from a pair of two-by-fours and some other scraps salvaged from the old barn.

"It's a good ladder," Jeff said when we finished.

I pushed the new ladder into the pit, and soon water was squirting from the brass valve, making our pump freezeproof. We replaced the cover on the well and mentally noted that several rotting boards should be replaced. Falling into the well pit could be dangerous and very painful.

The pump house needed cleaning too, a good project for next spring. Two swallow nests were firmly attached to two-by-four crosspieces; old newspapers were piled in one corner and old tin cans in another.

"The wagon shed doors are open," Steve said. "What're we gonna do with them?"

We propped scrap lumber against the doors to keep them shut.

Earlier we decided to leave some feed for rabbits and other animals that live around the buildings at Roshara. Through a board we pounded large nails about six inches apart. On the sharp ends of the nails the youngsters impaled ears of corn.

"What is gonna eat the corn?" Sue asked.

"Rabbits and squirrels, maybe even crows," I answered.

We placed the corn boards under the end willow, against the south side of the huge gnarled trunk. The willow trunk would be a protection from the cold north winds; wild animals could eat under the tree and be warmed by the winter sun. Near the end willow was a brush pile; rabbits might hide in the brushy tangle and be only a short distance from food.

Roshara was ready for winter. Except for the few morsels of food we left, the animals and birds would have to fend for themselves as they had done in previous winters. I was intensely interested in this struggle and in the cycles of their existence. Animals, land, and even I seemed immutably bound together. I wanted to return and be a part of it all, and listen and see.

One day in January I came back to Roshara by myself; Ruthie and the children stayed with Grandma and Grandpa.

It was a cold morning, twelve below zero, when I strapped on skis for my winter inspection. The snow was more than boot-top deep in many places, belt deep where the wind piled it against a fence or hedgerow.

Roshara's hills were white and quiet. The only sound was the scrape and crunch of skis as I pushed over the snow.

The pond was only a white depression in a white valley. The frozen pond rested for the long winter under the heavy snow until the sun and warm rains of March would dissolve the white cover and rot the ice. No deer tracks rimmed the pond as in fall. Now deer ate snow to obtain water.

I found rabbit tracks where cottontails had run from their hideout in a brush pile to a brushy area in search of food. The tracks also told where they had romped in the snow, playing winter rabbit games, and looked for tender twigs to nibble.

Then I skied up the hill, across an open field toward the oak wood lot. I crossed two deer tracks; the deer had walked slowly across the snow-swept fields.

The wood lot was nearly as silent as the open fields, except for the occasional snapping as the trees reported the cold that gripped their cells and expanded them rupturing the fibers. There was the dry, hollow, deathlike sound of brown oak leaves rubbing together, clinging still to their branches.

I stood motionless on the skis, listening. A lone woodpecker pounded for his breakfast of worms in a dead oak tree up the hill behind me. He too must have been cold, for the taps were carefully spaced, like a small boy with his first hammer trying to drive a nail into a board.

I followed a fox track out of the wood lot and into another field until it joined with another fox track. These tracks told a story of a search for food. Occasionally the snow was pushed aside where the foxes had dug into brown grass for field mice. The tracks also told of a time for play, where the foxes had rolled over and over in the snow, packing it hard.

Near the buildings I found another rabbit trail that led to the food we had placed under the end willow tree. The corncobs were red fingers on the board, the yellow kernels missing. The trail led from the food supply under the end willow to the nearby brush pile, and then into the wagon shed. Rabbits had found a crack in the door and had used the building as a winter home and, no doubt, a refuge from foxes who discovered the rabbit trails in the snow.

Alone on this cold winter day, I looked out over Roshara's snow-packed hills and thought of what this farm meant to me.

Here I could stand and think and make sense out of a hectic, hurried life. The seasons alter at Roshara as they have for thousands of years, never hurried, yet always changing. There is no hidden voice crying faster, faster, make spring come faster; hurry the year, send out blossoms sooner, melt the ice more quickly; woodpecker, pound faster; snake crawl more quickly; cricket, saw your legs faster, faster, hurry, hurry. Why hurry, nature asks. Why?

As I stood on that snow-swept hill on our Roshara, I thought, Why hurry? Why? Why must life move increasingly faster? And if it must—which I doubt—I'm thankful for this opportunity to see life move as it always has, slowly, deliberately, planned, unpressed to hurry. Thank God, the land still lives, I whispered.

XI

Winter

In February we again returned to Roshara. Above-freezing temperatures melted and packed the snow so it was heavily crusted and carried us on top.

We were concerned about the fish in our pond. Old-timers had predicted severe winterkilling of fish for much of Wisconsin, particularly in the smaller lakes. Heavy snow meant little chance for the sunlight to filter through the ice and provide life-giving light to the plants and oxygen to the fish.

Shallow lakes winterkill most often, and our pond averages less than six feet deep. I shoveled through eighteen inches of snow, then chopped through eighteen inches of slush ice and finally four inches of firm ice before water gushed up into the hole.

"Water's so black and dirty," Steve noted.

"Smells bad too," Sue said.

"Look at those frogs," Jeff said. Two dead and bloated

frogs floated to the surface. The stench of dead and decaying plants wafted around us.

The pond suffered a triple threat. First, the water area carrying dissolved oxygen decreased as the ice got thicker. Second, the weight of the deepening snow was pushing the ice down into the water. Third, the heavy snow blocked out the sunlight, without which water plants could not grow and produce oxygen. Furthermore, dead plants used up more oxygen as they decayed.

When the oxygen supply in a lake is short, the fish often rise toward the surface and live just under the ice. If any oxygen remains, that's where it's found.

But no fish came up into the hole, only dead frogs. We feared the worst, that the severe winter had killed our fish. But we wouldn't know for sure until spring when we could toss worm-baited hooks into the water.

A few weeks earlier, my brother Donald and his son Marc, from Sheboygan, were tramping the woods and found a deer yard—a place where many deer were wintering together. The deer had eaten the branches of the jack pine to a height of six feet from the ground, and they had nipped off the tips of every cherry and willow branch in the area. They had even pruned bur oak trees; some of the branches eaten were as thick as a man's little finger. The deer were starving.

The snow was so deep the deer traveled on a very

narrow trail that wound through the woods from one feeding area to another. They followed the same trail each day, and the food supply along the trail was entirely consumed.

Don told our neighbor Floyd Jeffers about it. "Those deer are starving," Don told Floyd, and he went on to explain what he'd seen in the woods.

"Think you're right, Don," said Floyd. "Ain't aware of deer yardin' up around here; thought they only did that in northern Wisconsin. Sounds bad. I'll see what I can do."

Floyd told Ollie Hansel from Wild Rose about the starving deer. Ollie had been feeding deer east of Wild Rose for several weeks.

On a March day when we were visiting Roshara, I walked out to the feeding area with Floyd. With a bale of hay on a small hand sleigh and a sack of ear corn over his back, he had been hauling feed this way since Don told him about the problem.

Soon we were at his feeding place, on the south side of a clump of jack pine trees. There was a sunny hillside where the deer could bed down and a jack pine clump for protection during cold windy weather.

The feeding area was like a barnyard. Cleanly eaten corncobs were scattered around as well as the stems of hay the deer had picked over.

"Funny thing about these deer," Floyd said. "They like

alfalfa and clover with lots of leaves. They don't like the stems."

"They appear kind of intelligent to me," I answered.

From what I could see, the deer had been smart enough to pick out the choicest parts of the hay and sleep on the stems.

"For a while I fed a bushel of corn every two or three days," Floyd said. "The animals were plenty weak when we first found 'em. Didn't try to move away from their heavily traveled trail at all. Lots of browse a few feet from the trail, but the deer were just too weak to get to it."

Then Floyd said proudly, "We ain't found any dead ones yet, so we musta got to 'em in time."

There were fringe benefits to the feeding. As Floyd and I walked around the feeding area, we noticed several bluejays and a half-dozen chickadees enjoying the handouts. Squirrel and rabbit tracks covered the snow.

That afternoon Ollie Hansel arrived at the farm with his snowmobile. Ollie had another feeding area farther up in the woods.

We hitched Ollie's larger sled to the snowmobile before throwing on a bale of hay and a gunny sack of ear corn. The yellow snowmobile sputtered into life the second time Ollie pulled the cord. "Climb on," Ollie said, and we glided down the hill toward the pond and onto the far side of the valley.

When we stopped and were unloading the feed, I asked Ollie how he got started feeding deer. He spent two days a week distributing food and received no pay.

In his unassuming manner he replied, "Well, I guess it started last fall, when I left uncut a small cornfield for the deer." Ollie farmed part time besides operating the auto body shop in Wild Rose.

"Soon after Christmas the corn was gone, and I knew I'd have to keep feeding 'em. There's been seven deer comin' to that field all winter. Then word got around. Farmers'd tell me where they were finding deer near starvation and I'd go out and feed 'em."

We carried the corn and hay a short distance into the woods while Ollie continued his story. "One place east of Wild Rose I feed I'd guess forty deer, another place maybe thirty, and the rest of the places probably as many as twenty. I started doin' it on snowshoes pullin' a small sled, like Floyd does. But that was too much work. It took too much time too, especially as the snow got deeper. So I bought this snowmobile; makes the job a lot easier. Farmers gave me the corn and hay, and some people even gave me money to buy feed," he said.

We followed the deer trail up the hill in the woods. The trail was well packed, narrow, and eighteen inches deep in the snow. We found many shrubs near the trail that the deer hadn't touched.

"For some reason they won't go off the trail," Ollie said. "They follow the same trail day after day, around in a big circle. They won't get off it even if there's something to eat only a few feet away."

We walked back toward the snowmobile and found a clearing in the woods that the deer trail crossed. "This looks like a good place to leave feed," Ollie said as he grabbed the bale of hay and I grabbed the sack of corn.

"Should I dump the corn?"

"No, you'd better scatter it around or they'll fight for it, and the little deer always lose."

The feed scattered, we climbed back on the snow-mobile and soon were back on the road.

While we were loading the snowmobile on Ollie's truck, I asked him why he fed deer.

"Well, somebody's gotta do it or we'd have a lot of dead deer, and if not dead deer the females will drop dead fawns this spring. Besides, I kinda enjoy gettin' out in the woods." He waved out the window of his pickup and drove on to the next feeding spot on his circuit.

Later in the winter, we returned to Roshara to clean out the pump house. It was an above-freezing day; though soggy on top, the snow still was more than three feet deep around the buildings.

The boys helped carry out the pile of old newspapers stashed in the corner of the pump house, *Milwaukee Sen-*

*tinel*s dated 1957. After removing the top layers of newspapers, Steve stopped. "These papers are all chewed up," he said.

Deer mice had found a home in the old papers. Toward the center of the pile we found the mouse nest fabricated from small bits of shredded paper arranged in a ball about four inches across.

We started a fire on top of the snow with the mice-infested newspapers; the mice were gone, of course. The fire burned rapidly and soon melted through the many layers of snow and came to rest on the bare ground. Later, when the fire was out, we looked at the hole.

As the rings of a tree record its growth, the snow profile summarized the winter. A thick ring of snow between two layers of ice recalled the Christmas blizzard when cars were stranded and holiday travelers changed plans. A ring of ice told of the thaw in January that settled the snow, leaving a dark gray streak in the profile.

The fire hole in the snow reminded me of a pit in the ground; the various layers of soil told something of how the soil was formed, what the glacier left, and how the organic material accumulated in the top inches over the years.

XII

Recalling the Past

When we cleaned out the pump house we found the potato planter John and Weston Coombes had used to put seed potatoes in the ground each spring. The metal end that opened the hole in the soil was rusted dark brown.

I recalled the stories of John Coombes with his team, old Duke and Queenie, plowing the fields each spring. In the early 1900s potatoes were an important cash crop in the sandy area of central Wisconsin. The soil was naturally acid, ideal for potato growing. On the richer, less acid soils of the southern parts of the state, potatoes developed scabby blotches on their skins and were less valuable.

As soon as the frost was out of the ground and the land firm enough to hold horses and plow, John plowed the sandy soil, as much as ten acres of it, for a potato crop. He liked the smell of freshly turned soil as he held the handles of the walking plow and followed in the furrow.

At most he could plow two acres a day, often less if hot

weather came early. Hot weather quickly tired Duke and Queenie as they trudged up and down the gently rolling hills. The furrows were straight and true, the mark of a good plowman. Years later John would learn that had he plowed around rather than up and down the hills, they would have kept their fertility and the gullies wouldn't have formed.

The previous fall John seeded rye in the cornfields after harvest. The rye was a luxuriant green in contrast to the drab fields not yet awakened from their winter dormancy.

After plowing, John hitched his team to a disc and smoothed the furrows. Clouds of dust rose from behind the disc as the sandy soil quickly dried in the spring sun.

John next marked the soil with a wooden marker that etched six straight lines in the soft sand. He drove the marker, pulled by old Queenie, both ways on the field. Where the lines crossed, John planted his crop. The rows were thirty-six inches apart, spaced evenly in both directions so potatoes would grow as if on a giant checkerboard.

Meanwhile, Ina and the children cut the seed potatoes into chunks, making sure there was at least one eye on each piece.

With potato bags over their shoulders, John and Weston walked along the straight marks, lifting the potato planter, dropping in a piece of cut potato from the bag, shoving the planter into the ground, and then dragging one foot to cover the hole. Weston was always barefoot, except when he planted potatoes. Then he wore a shoe on his "draggin' foot," which otherwise would have become skinned and bruised as it dragged in the warm, soft soil. People often wondered why the right shoe worn by central Wisconsin farm boys was more worn than the left. Anyone who had watched potato planting had the answer.

A few days after the field was seeded John hitched one horse to the walking cultivator and followed it up and down the rows, using the marks as guides. It would be two weeks or more before the green shoots of new potato plants pushed through the sandy soil. Ragweed grew much faster than potatoes and had to be controlled.

Through the warm days of early summer, John and Weston cultivated and hoed the potatoes. The amount of rainfall determined whether they would get seventy-five bushels per acre or two hundred.

Weather was desperately important in their lives. John and Weston watched the sunset each night and made folkish predictions about the following day's weather.

"Sky in the west is red; tomorrow's gonna be fair!"

"Them little dimples of clouds . . . they mean rain'll come in twenty-four hours."

"Red sky at mornin', Weston, sailors take warnin'."

They watched wind direction too. A south or west

wind usually meant fair weather, but an east wind could mean rain. John and Weston often went to bed hoping for storm clouds that never developed. Each day in August they watched the corn leaves curl and shrivel. With a prolonged drought, the lower leaves turned brown and dried up. If the drought continued for more than two weeks, the corn plants on the hilltops completely dried up and rattled hopelessly as the hot winds moved over the fields.

Lack of rain in July and August was always a problem. The corn needed rain to develop well-filled ears; the potatoes needed rain to round out large, mature tubers.

Potato bugs could also ruin a crop. While hoeing potatoes, John looked carefully for the bright orange, soft-shelled bugs. He tried to spot them while they were little, the size of a kitchen match head or smaller. If allowed to grow they would strip the leaves down to the bare jagged stems. Then the plants would die.

There were always a few potato bugs, but an excessive number necessitated killing them with a Paris Green mixture. John bought the Paris Green at Hotz Brothers Hardware in Wild Rose, mixed it with water, and then shook it on the potato plants with a hazel branch. Some years he used a broom made from marsh hay tied to a stick, but marsh hay wasn't always available, as none grew on the farm.

Once the crows prevented a crop failure. There were

thousands of crows in Skunk's Hollow. In the early morning they flew toward the east, crying for food. Later in the afternoon they flew back west, into the deep woods to roost.

That year tobacco worms invaded the Coombeses' potato field. "They'll wipe out the entire crop," John cried desperately. "I don't know how we can get rid of 'em."

Then the crows discovered the tobacco worms. To John, it was like a miracle. Thousands of crows flocked to the field and walked up and down the green rows of potatoes snapping the worms from the leaves. In three days the field was free of worms and John's opinion of crows had changed, at least for a few days. "Them wonderful black devils," he said.

Crows had always been his enemy, for they destroyed crops too. When the new corn was an inch tall, crows often walked the rows, grabbing the tender corn plants in their bills, uprooting the entire plant.

John had a solution to this problem. He seized his double-barrelled shotgun from its nail in the living room and blasted one of the crows. Then he hung the dead bird from a tall stick in the middle of the cornfield.

"Darnedest thing happened," he said. "Blamed crows seemed to come from everywhere to pay last respects to the dead. Like they was havin' a funeral! Cawed around for more'n an hour. Made a terrible racket. Then them crows just up and flew away—didn't bother my cornfield anymore."

The potato harvest started in late September. With a six-tined barn fork, John walked backward down the row of potatoes and dug each hill, shaking loose the large red potatoes from the mature and dying tops. The red varieties, King, Early Rose, and Stray Beauty, did best on the sandy soil. It was years later that the white varieties became popular.

Following their father, Weston and Charlotte filled pails with potatoes and dumped them into wooden bushel-size potato boxes. It took many days to dig ten acres of potatoes; the digging season often went into late October, when fingers numbed picking up the potatoes and the digger with the fork moved mighty fast to keep warm.

When part of the potatoes were dug, John hitched Duke and Queenie to the high-wheeled wagon loaded with fifty bushels of freshly dug spuds and headed for Wild Rose. There were bills to pay—seed, groceries, farm equipment.

The wheels of the loaded wagon often cut a foot deep into the sandy road. On his way to Wild Rose, John passed his neighbors, Frank Darling, Art Stewart, and Fremont Jeffers.

"Looks like you got a crop," Frank yelled.

"Always do," John hollered back.

"Them crows help you out this year?"

"Ain't seen a blessed crow," cried John.

He drove his wagon past Chain O' Lake, the largest lake of many in the area, past the Chain O' Lake School, and then he turned onto the road from the west that would take him to town. People still called the road the old Indian trail.

John passed Lizzie Ratliff's place and John Jenks's farm before resting the team in front of Jessie DeWitt's place. Jessie came out to the road.

"Potato prices are low this fall, John," Jessie said.

"I know," John said, "but bills gotta be paid. I'll sell 'em for what I can get."

Next was Amel Hansel's place and then Tom Lowe's; on the corner on top of a hill lived the Otto Gabrielskis. Here the road turned south for a quarter-mile, and on the corner, where it turned east again, lived the Gordon Darlings. Then came the Will Darling and Jim Larson farms.

On the other side of a long sandy hill lived Andrew Etheridge on the right and Otto Radloff on the left, then Jerry Pierce and finally Jeff Sage.

John knew them all. It was like driving through a whole country of old friends.

John crossed the Chicago & North Western Railroad tracks, passed the railroad stockyard with its bawling cattle, and turned onto the Wautoma road that drilled into Wild Rose.

Potato buyers waited alongside the Wautoma road to meet the potato wagons as they entered town. John yelled "whoa" to Duke and Queenie, and two potato buyers climbed on the wagon to inspect his load.

"I'll give ya thirty cents a bushel," one said.

"I'll make it thirty-two," the second buyer offered.

"Thirty-five cents is my top price," the first buyer said as he jumped down from the wagon.

"Too much for me," said the second buyer, and he turned his attention to another wagon coming down the sandy road.

There were potato warehouses all along the railroad tracks—the Stark Brothers, the Penny Company, H. Stedman and Sons, E. R. Kelley, T. S. Chittendon and Melcher.

The potato buyer directed John to the Stark Brothers warehouse, and he drove his wagon onto their scale. The load of potatoes, John, and team were weighed. After the potatoes were unloaded, the empty wagon, John, and the horses were weighed again. The buyer wrote the difference in weight on a weigh check and handed it to John.

John drove his team to the bank, tied them in front while he went inside, and waited for Jim Burns, the banker, to figure out how many bushels of potatoes he had sold. The scaler at the warehouse had written only the number of pounds of potatoes and the price per bushel. His figuring finished, the banker gave John $17.50 in cash.

"A lot of money, John," Jim said.

"Ain't much for all my work, me and my boy," John said.

Wild Rose was a busy potato town. Each season 650 boxcar loads of potatoes were shipped south to Chicago. The village had grown to 551 people in 1910 and was a major trading center.

From the bank John went to Patterson's General Store to pay his grocery bill. Patterson had a large hitching rail behind his store, and fifteen other potato wagons and teams stood waiting.

All the services a potato farmer could want were in the village. There was Keppler's Harness Shop, Bob K. Jones's Hardware, T. W. Stevens's Drugstore, Oscar Holt's General Store, Hanna and Margaret Bowen's Millinery Shop, Lant Etheridge's Blacksmith Shop, William Jones's Furniture Store, Upton's Hotel, Fred Clark's Grocery, Frank Clark's Drugstore, C. A. Smart's General Store, and Walter Walters's Implement Store. There was Benjamin's restaurant and pool hall, a barbershop, a creamery, a dentist's office, the livery stable, and Hoaglin's Mill.

Pine River was dammed at Hoaglin's Mill, and the millpond paralleled the town's sandy main street. Besides grinding flour and cow feed, the mill also provided electricity for the village. At midnight the mill shut down and the electricity went out until the next morning when the water wheel started turning again. The water wheel had to be stopped each night to give the millpond a chance to rise and provide enough water to run the water wheel the following day. Whenever anyone in Wild Rose had a party, it ended before midnight or the party-goers had to get out old kerosene lamps.

John hauled as many loads of potatoes to Wild Rose as it took to pay his bills. The remaining potatoes he buried in pits in the fields and covered them with soil and horse manure to keep them from freezing. Late in the fall, before snow, he would dig them up and sell them. Potatoes sold early brought as little as twenty-five cents a bushel; later they might bring a dollar. It paid to gamble that the weather wouldn't get cold enough to freeze the potatoes in the ground.

Before all the potatoes were dug, John and Weston harvested their few rows of sweet sorghum. If the sorghum froze, the sweet juice soured. They stripped the leaves from the stalks with a board sharpened like a knife, then cut off the tops. The sorghum was hauled to a sorghum mill at Wild Rose where the slender canes were fed between two spring-loaded rollers that squeezed out the juice.

The press was powered by a small gasoline engine so only four or five sorghum stalks could be fed into the rollers at a time. The juice ran down a metal trough into a two-hundred-gallon tank. With wooden buckets, the juice was dipped from the tank into an evaporating pan ten feet long, four feet wide, and a foot deep.

A crackling wood fire heated the juice in the pan until it boiled. Clouds of sweet-smelling steam rolled out from under the roof of the sorghum shed; there were no ends on the building, and the sides were open as well. Long pieces of oak were continuously shoved into the fire to keep the juice boiling. Occasionally a bubbly scum was skimmed from the surface of the juice with a stick, a board nailed on the end.

After about two hours, the juice was transferred to a second vat that was the same size but had a slower fire. Gradually the clear juice turned thicker and golden brown. After three hours in the second vat, the golden liquid, about the consistency of warm molasses, was dipped into milk cans. Rich and sweet, it had an aroma that could make any farmer hungry.

During the winter the Coombes family poured the sorghum on bread and pancakes or used it to make candy and to flavor baked beans. According to a countryside belief, consuming plenty of sorghum even helped prevent rheumatism!

People said Indians drank the juice squeezed from cornstalks. But no one knew how the Indians fixed the juice before they drank it. Because corn is a relative of sorghum, they believed sorghum must have the same virtues as corn juice, and of course corn juice properly prepared—well, dynamite was safer.

We often found effects that elicited the past. Hanging from a nail in the pumphouse were the rusty plates from John Coombes's horse-drawn corn planter.

The plates fit in the bottom of the corn boxes on the planter and carefully spaced the dropping of kernels into the soil. The horse-drawn planter was a vast improvement over the hand corn planter. The farmer could plant two rows of corn at once and ride on the planter too.

A crooked-handled rake leaned against the pump house wall, the rake end wired firmly in place. No doubt this was the rake Mrs. Coombes used each spring to clean up around her house. To keep the house warm, the Coombeses piled straw around the foundation each fall, then raked it into piles and hauled it away in the spring.

Half a bundle of unused cedar shingles Weston Coombes had used for patching holes in the roofs lay in one corner. Although it was many years old, when I held a shingle close I could detect still the sweet fragrance of cedar.

We found several pails of rusty nails and half a bag of cement long ago hardened to the consistency of granite.

But the important find of the day, at least to Ruthie,

was an antique jug, a two-gallon size, dark brown on the top and lighter tan on the sides, with an opening large enough to accept a corncob. It was the jug John Coombes might have used to carry cool water to the hayfields. On the other hand, the jug might have held something stronger.

We found the jug not in the pump house but in a place where most people wouldn't look for it.

One of the cleanup tasks that day was to get rid of the old outhouse that stood underneath the willow trees, almost hidden by the trees and shrubs in summer. We'd decided to burn the building where it stood rather than try to tear it down.

I tucked a few newspapers inside the door, squirted a little coal oil on the papers, and struck a match. The dry old wood snapped and cracked wildly as the furious flames consumed it. Finally the frame settled to the ground. Snow kept the fire from spreading.

When the outhouse was a pile of ashes, the brown jug was revealed. The fire hadn't damaged it, but we let the jug cool slowly so it wouldn't crack.

Why was the jug hidden behind the outhouse? And what had been in it? You might assume that an earlier resident at Roshara kept his whisky there, away from those whose faces turned grim at any mention of strong drink.

When the jug cooled enough, we each took a whiff. Ruthie thought there just might have been whisky in it. To me it smelled like coal oil. "Castor oil," Steve cried. "Honey!" yelled Sue. "This musta been a honey jug!"

We had a great time imagining what the jug had contained. And we cherished the jug because it belonged, because it was part of the story, and because it was ours.

XIII

Roshara's Birds

April. Warm winds from the south wash over Roshara's hills and life begins again. The wrens are back in the willow trees, the bluebirds have made their nests. The barn swallows fly in and out of the granary, where their nest is firmly attached to a ceiling joist. A robin couple shares the pump house with a pair of barn swallows.

The first sprigs of green grass push through the tangle of dried and matted mulch left when the heavy snows packed flat last summer's growth.

The ice on the pond is gone and the water is high, the highest since we've owned Roshara. We get wet feet when we walk in the grass close to the pond's edge; last year we walked there in dry comfort. We must get out fish poles soon to see if winter killed the fish.

It's a weekend to put up more birdhouses. Steve and I have worked several evenings making wren and bluebird houses from a four-by-eight sheet of outdoor plywood.

I sawed the pieces and Steve nailed them together. We made three houses for wrens and two for bluebirds; Steve is eager to see if they will attract the birds they were designed for.

We walk down the trail toward the pond, Steve and I, then turn into the open field to the south. An old dividing fence, long since collapsed and broken except for two sturdy cedar posts, is our goal. We fasten a shiny green bluebird house to each.

"Do you think bluebirds will find them?" Steve asks.

"I doubt it," I answer. "I think we're a little late for bluebirds this year. I'd guess they've already nested."

"They gonna be empty then, Dad?"

"We'll wait and see. Maybe some other bird will like what we've made."

We walk back to the buildings where we plan to hang the wren houses. As we pass last year's tin can houses, we see sticks poking out the holes. Wrens have found them. Wrens chatter in the trees as we wire two new houses to limbs in the willows. The third one we wire onto the lower branch of an elm tree alongside the driveway. We'd run out of green paint so this one has a red roof.

"Let's look in the granary," Steve says. He wants to see the barn swallow nest I've told him about.

The beautiful, steel blue swallow chirp sharply, warningly as we enter. I know she is setting on white eggs speckled with dots of red, brown, and lavender. Her cinnamon brown breast is nearly hidden.

Another swallow nest is in the beginning stages; only the mud base is there. Steve and I sit outside the granary watching the fork-tailed birds carry mud in their beaks, less than half a teaspoon per trip.

"Where they gettin' the mud?" Steve asks.

"Oh, probably near the pond."

Occasionally the birds carry blades of dried grass to reinforce the mud. Slowly the nest takes shape as we watch. When the mud base is about six inches square, the swallows carry dried grass to build on the foundation. When finished, the nest will be as large as my two fists and lined with feathers.

"How come swallows make a nest like that, Dad?"

"Don't know, Steve, don't think anybody knows. They've just always done it that way."

A little later, when we walk to the car, a wren is sitting on top of the house with the red roof.

"Gee, they like it, the wrens like our house!" Steve cries. As he speaks, the wren slides through the hole into the wren house. Instant success. We are proud of our house-building efforts, especially Steve. He figures he is now a wren expert, and that the red roof is his special invention and recipe for success.

But I was right about the bluebirds. We were too late

with the wooden houses. An inspection of the new houses on our next visit to Roshara, however, shows that a tree swallow has nested in each one.

"Pretty good houses, huh, Dad?" Steve says. "I knew we'd get tree swallows." I can see that Steve is taking over as our birdhouse man.

A tree swallow sits on the roof of the house closest to us, its back the same steel blue color as a barn swallow, but its breast snow white, not cinnamon brown. All of the wooden wren houses are filled; the willow windbreak is a chorus of wren song, each singing to drown out his or her neighbor and all adding a melodious dimension to our farm visits. Wrens must have problems too, yet they are always singing, always happy. I think about pointing this out as a family object lesson but decide to save my moralizing for a more desperate occasion.

The bluebirds haven't chosen our new houses, but we often see a pair sitting on the fence near the buildings. We surmise a natural bluebird nest is nearby since bluebirds are territorial minded, each male mapping out and protecting a territory around his mate's nest.

"That's the prettiest bird I've ever seen," Sue says as we stand that afternoon watching the male on the wire fence. Indeed, the bright blue back contrasting with the orange breast is a strikingly beautiful color combination for any living creature.

"Look!" Sue says, pointing to the end willow. "He flew into that tree. See, he's sitting on that broken limb."

And then the bluebird vanishes. Slowly, Sue and I walk to the tree, our eyes fixed on the stub branch. Could it be that what looked like a woodpecker hole in the dead stub was a nesting site? Impossible. According to the books I've read, bluebirds preferred the open fields, away from trees and buildings. First choice for a bluebird nest, according to my bird book, is a hollow wooden fence post. Nest in a tree? Never. The dead branch is at least ten feet from the ground and it surely is not in the open.

But there is a bluebird nest in the woodpecker hole, and baby bluebirds too. We move away from the tree and watch the male and female make repeated trips to the nest in the hollow limb, each time carrying a bug or food of some kind to their hungry babies.

We've never watched bluebirds so close or seen them caring for their young in natural surroundings. Whenever we aren't doing something else that weekend, we watch the bluebirds. No human entertainment, we think, could compare with this production sponsored by nature.

A few weeks earlier I had observed another strange nesting place. My brother Donald, who has a private plane license, had flown with his family to Wautoma. We drove him back to the airstrip and watched him go through his preflight checks before takeoff.

"The instructor said always to check around the engine whenever you park the plane overnight," Don said.

"What do you expect to find?" I asked.

"Bird's nest. If there's one there and you don't find it, you could be in for some trouble once you get into the air and the engine overheats."

"Ever find a nest?" I asked.

"Nope, but once is too many times."

He lifted the engine cover and there it was, a nearly completed wren's nest, built against the air intake.

"Well, I'll be. Instructor said birds would nest there because it's warm. Never thought I'd find one though," Don said.

We removed two handfuls of wren nest. No doubt there was a very frustrated wren when she returned to find that her newly found nesting site had flown away.

But wrens will build almost anywhere. When I was a boy, one wren insisted on building a nest in our farm mailbox. Every day when we went for the mail, we removed the nest, and the next day there would be a new one. After a week of this put and take, the wren gave up and looked for another nesting place.

When we visited Canada a few years ago, we saw a swallow nest built above the men's washroom on the ferry that went from the mainland to an island several miles out in Lake Winnipeg. The swallow was sitting on its nest, not the least bit nervous about its high mobility. Perhaps the floating home provided some food sources not available on the mainland.

Barn swallows nest in the granary, of course, two sets of them. How will we move them from the granary when we start working on it? How do you evict a swallow family without breaking up a home?

I think how the young swallows had been accidentally killed when the old barn fell in on them. The children will never forgive me if I kill any more swallows.

XIV

Cabin Plans

To remodel the old granary we had to tear out the manure-encrusted wood on the inside and brush down the dusty cobwebs that stuck to our faces when we walked into them.

And, of course, we must sweep the dirt from the cracked concrete floor.

Armed with a wrecking bar, I started on the horse mangers that were firmly nailed to the north wall. Ancient timothy hay half-filled them as if Weston Coombes's two horses were only temporarily away, let out into the barnyard to exercise. Surely they'd return shortly to finish eating.

But it had been nearly five years since Weston's horses had stood in this corner of the old granary, pawing the concrete floor and biting the manger boards. Some say horses bite wood when they lack minerals in their diet; others claim they do it to break the monotony of standing tied in one place.

I pounded loose the top board, and a puff of timothy dust made me sneeze. The dust got thicker in the granary as I pounded loose other boards and piled them near the door. Occasionally, I retreated outside to fill my lungs with clean air and polish the dust from my glasses.

After the manger was apart, I knocked the boards from the partition that had held oats or rye in one corner of the building. More dust.

I pried loose the wood lath that held black tar paper against the inside wall. When Weston turned the granary into a horse barn he nailed tar paper to the walls to plug the mouse and rat holes and keep out the winter winds. Behind the tar paper I found mouse nests, bits of hay and straw formed into ragged balls.

By evening my eyes were red and sore, and my head felt as though I'd contracted a severe cold. But I knew the symptoms were caused by the dust that was flying everywhere.

As I stood in the doorway of the granary I tried to visualize how it might transform into a cabin. The door could be boarded up and another door cut into the chicken house to give us more room. We could replace the little barn window on the east end with a narrow sliding window and put a kitchen sink under it.

But I stopped. Ruthie must be consulted, and just maybe we should get a carpenter's opinion too. There was likely to be a difference between what we wanted to do and what was possible. The wooden walls were in poorer condition than I first thought. With the tar paper removed, sunlight streamed through the boards everywhere, lighting the dust particles in the air and sending shafts of light bouncing off the floor.

Maybe the granary wasn't worth remodeling. Perhaps only a barn it was and would always be, never a cabin.

But the swallows liked it; even with the pounding and dust they continued caring for their babies in the nests. Occasionally they scolded and flew around my head when I came too close to their nests, but they gave no indication of leaving.

I crawled up the shaky ladder with an old broom and some liquid detergent. Did we need a new floor upstairs too? I scrubbed through fifty-seven years of dust and dirt until I got through to the bare floor.

The floor was beautiful. It was matched pine lumber aged to a shimmering soft brown, darker where there were knots. It was sound, good as new, but it needed several more scrubbings before we could sleep on it. The floor shook some when I walked across it; a beam placed against the ceiling joists downstairs would correct the problem. Surely a beam had been salvaged from the old barn.

Over the long Fourth of July weekend we again camped at Roshara. While the children climbed in the end willow and played on the rope swing, Ruthie and I scrubbed the inside of the granary. With water and disinfectant we attacked the downstairs wall, every board and every two-by-four. We scrubbed the ceiling boards and every fly-specked two-by-eight ceiling joist until Ruthie cried in despair, "We'll never get it clean! It's impossible to wash a horse barn."

It seemed so to me, too.

It was hot and humid in the granary as we stood on stepladders with disinfectant water running down our sleeves and soaking our clothing. Slowly the aroma in the granary changed from horse smell to disinfectant smell, from a musty smell to a clean, fresh smell. But it was slow, wet, hot work.

There was one swallow nest with the young not quite ready to leave. We scrubbed up to the nest on the ceiling joist, went past it, and scrubbed on the other side. The swallow scolded but kept carrying food to her young. The baby birds nearly filled the nest. We tore down the other vacant swallow habitation and washed away the dried mud where it had hung.

Floyd Jeffers came over to see what we were doing. "Doubt you folk'll ever get out all the horse smell," he said cheerfully. "I suppose it's seeped into the grain of the wood. Probably into the concrete floor too. Scrubbin' should help though."

"Have to wait and see," I told him. "Sure hope the place has a different smell when it dries out. But at least it'll be clean."

"Well, you're clean city folks. Don't blame you none!"

We wanted professional advice from a carpenter before we worked any more. Was the building structurally sound?

"Why don't you ask Ole Knutson to come out and have a look at the granary?" my father said. "He's a carpenter, you know, worked in Chicago for years. He'll tell you if the granary is worth working on."

We were at work when Ole drove out to Roshara from Wild Rose where he lived.

"Name's Ole Knutson," he said as we met in front of the granary. "Hear you're plannin' to make this old building into a cabin." Ole was more than six feet tall, had broad shoulders, and wore dark-rimmed glasses. At seventy years old, he walked so vigorously we thought he was ten years younger.

"We're thinking about it, Ole," I answered. "But we need somebody like you to look at it. Hate to sink any money if the place isn't basically sound."

"Well, let's have a look," Ole said as he walked into the granary. "Looks like you've been doing some cleaning. Heard there were horses in here. Sometimes hard to get horse smell out of an old building like this, but you've got the right idea. A good scrubbin'll help, and when you get some new lumber in here, I don't think you'll smell the horses anymore."

"That's good!" Ruthie said. "People have told us the place would always smell like a horse barn."

Ole unfolded his rule and measured the length and width. "Fourteen by twenty, good size for a cabin, especially with an upstairs."

He looked at the foundation. "When was this building built?"

"About 1912, so I've heard."

"Gotta hand it to those carpenters; they built a good wall under this place. Lots of carpenters set the sill on stones, or even on the ground. But you've got a concrete wall, and the sill doesn't seem to be rottin' at all."

He looked upstairs. "Floor seems all right up here. Course you'll need to insulate the roof and put in some windows to give you more light. And you'll need a new stairway. You'd kill yourself on this old ladder."

"What about the floor downstairs? What should we do with that?"

"That's easy. Just put another floor right over the top; the ceiling's high enough to do that."

Then Ole looked at the outside and shook his head. "Here's your biggest problem," he said. "If they'd only painted the siding. Look at this—too rotten to save, too many holes in it. The water'll run in and spoil the inside. I think you oughta put on some new siding."

"Just a minute now, Ole," I said. "Are you saying the granary is worth fixing?"

"Sure is, no question about that. I've seen new buildings that ain't built as well as this granary. Course you've got some work here, lots of it."

I was reluctant to ask the next question. "Say, Ole, how about hiring you to help us?"

"Nope, not me. I can't work. Look at my hands, arthritis. I can barely hold a hammer anymore. Hands ache so I can't sleep. That's why I quit my job in Chicago, couldn't stand it with these bum hands."

"We're kinda stuck, Ole," I said. "I don't know a thing about carpentry. Do you suppose you could tell me what to do?"

"That I can do, by golly. I'll make you a deal seein' as how you're kinda stuck and carpenters are hard to come by, especially in the summer. I'll help with the measurin' and kinda tell you what to do every day, then I'll go back to town, and you can work. How'd that be?"

We were pleased, especially Ruthie; she knew what a poor carpenter I was. Ruthie had given me a handyman's book several weeks before, but she still doubted that I could translate the printed page into new doors and windows.

"When you gonna start this project?" Ole asked.

"In three weeks, when my vacation starts."

"All right, I'll be out the first day of your vacation. In the meantime, why don't you order some windows from the lumberyard so they'll be here when we're ready to go to work." He told me what sizes he thought I should order.

"You know, Ruthie," I said, after Ole had left, "I think we'll have a cabin after all, and it's not going to cost us a whole lot either."

"It's cost me quite a bit," Ruthie said, looking at her ruined hands.

"Whatever it costs," I said, "I think it'll be worth it. It's like bringing a dead thing back to life again. It's like the land—as though this old building was dead and suddenly it has a new purpose. I wish I could say it better . . ."

"You don't have to," Ruthie replied.

"I guess I don't."

XV

Floyd

It was again August and vacation time. We hauled our camping equipment to Roshara and, as before, pitched the tent in the shade of the end willow. Before the tent was up the children were playing on their rope swing and climbing in the tree.

It was a Saturday, and Ole had promised to come out on Monday morning. Later that morning my father came down to Roshara with his tractor and mower.

"I'll cut some of this tall grass around the buildings; kids won't get so wet when they play in the mornin'. Lots of dew on the grass these days. Think I'll cut a swath down to the pond, too—be easier to go fishin' then."

After cutting the grass around the buildings, he followed the trail to the pond and cut grass on the north side. He had driven in the same place other years, but this year there was almost a disaster.

What he failed to consider was the high water this

year and the muskrat tunnel under the bank on the north side. A back wheel broke through into a muskrat tunnel and the machine was stuck. "Get off the tractor, get off the tractor!" I yelled. "It's tipping into the pond."

The sickle bar of the mower kept it from tipping, but the tractor sank deeper into the soft soil each second.

"Think the sickle bar will hold it?" I asked nervously.

"I think so, but we'd better figure a way to get it out before it sinks any farther in the mud," Father said.

I ran up the hill to get Dad's pickup back at the granary along with some heavy wooden blocks and Dad's hydraulic building jack we planned to use to put the support beam in the granary.

But I drove too close to the tractor with the truck and it too was suddenly stuck and sinking into the mud. The entire north end of the pond was soggy and, as we learned too late, no place to drive.

"We've gotta have help," my father said. "The tractor looks like it'll flip over. The wheel in the muskrat runway is sinkin' faster than the other. If it dumps into the pond we'll never get it out. Pond's more'n four feet deep here."

Dad took my car and got Ronald Jennings, a neighbor, to come with his tractor and chain.

"Got yourself in quite a mess," Ronald observed as he stopped his tractor on safe high ground. "Don't know's I can pull her out, but at least I can keep the tractor from tippin' into the pond. Truck looks the easiest—let's start with that."

We hitched the chain to the truck frame, and slowly Jennings's tractor eased it out of the mud onto high ground.

"Now let's try your tractor. Don't know's I can move it—stuck pretty bad." He hooked the chain to the front axle. Slowly the chain tightened, but the tractor wasn't moving. On high ground it growled louder and then the wheel in the muskrat runway turned and came slowly out.

"What can I pay you, Ronald?" I asked.

"Forget it, sometime maybe I'll need some help," Ronald said. He drove out the driveway fast, perhaps afraid I'd offer again to pay him.

We sat for a few minutes to think about what had happened.

"Guess we were lucky. Could have lost the tractor," Father said.

"Good thing Ronald Jennings was home and could come."

Later that afternoon I suggested to the children that we go fishing. "There isn't much work we can do on the granary until Ole gets here."

We dug worms and walked to the pond. The youngsters unwound their poles and we baited hooks, but the shiny bobbers lay motionless on the pond's smooth surface. This was the answer to the question about the winter freeze and whether the fish had survived. The heavy snows had taken their toll. No fish were attacking the wiggly worms today.

"Look at that, Dad," Jeff said. He pointed to a small school of tiny bullheads. At least they had survived the long winter. But what about the bluegills and sunfish? Were they all dead?

On Sunday afternoon Ruthie and the children went swimming at Silver Lake. I stayed at Roshara to get the four-by-four beam ready to install on Monday morning. Ole had agreed that the beam would help stiffen the upstairs floor.

The beam had been a support beam in the old barn, oak, beautifully grained and solid, but dirty and covered with fly specks. I was scrubbing the beam when Floyd Jeffers came ambling down the drive.

"What're you up to today, Jerry?"

I told him about my plans for the beam. "Wonder if that beam wasn't from the old Tom Stewart house that stood across the road from my place. The first buildings weren't here but across the drive, right in front of my house. When they tore those buildings down some of the lumber went into the new barn."

He scratched his thumbnail on the beam. "Doubt this was in the old house though; those buildings were mostly pine, and this is oak."

"Say, Floyd, what do you know about the well on this place?"

"Oh, I'd say you've got about fifty-five feet to water, probably have to go another twenty or thirty feet to get what you'd call good water. Could be you'll have a problem with that well. Bottom end may be at a depth where red clay seeps through the screen and makes the water red and not fit to drink."

"Water is sort of red right now," I said.

"Course it could be rust that's causing it. Pump needs lots of pumpin' right now. Can't be sure if you've got a problem until you pump it enough to get rid of the rust. Talkin' about pumps, did ya hear that well driller poundin' away yesterday?" Floyd asked.

"I wondered what that boom-boom noise was."

"Three brothers bought the property just west of you, and each is plannin' to build a house. First one is goin' up right now. You know, they had electricity brought in for more'n half a mile. Clear from County O."

"How much is it going to cost us for electricity?" I asked. We had no electricity at Roshara but planned to have it brought into the cabin in a few years.

"Oh, not very much, something like thirty-six dollars a year whether you use it or not. Course if you use more'n a certain amount you pay more. Doubt electric co-op makes very much money on this type of electrical hookup. I'm sure it costs them several hundred dollars to set new poles and to string lines."

Talk got around to trees, and I showed Floyd the three soft maples I planted near the pump house. The trees had self-seeded from a soft maple tree in our back yard in Madison, and I transplanted them at Roshara.

"Looks like two of the three are gonna make it," Floyd commented. "This one looks dead, but you won't know 'til next spring. Say, how those pine trees doin' you planted?"

"Haven't had a chance to see them lately. Let's walk out and have a look."

In the hollow near the road, where the soil is richer and the quack grass more rank, the pine trees were having difficulty growing. They were fighting with the quack grass for light and nutrients, not losing the battle but not winning either.

Once the pines have grown enough to be above the grass they will grow rapidly. Eventually, when they are taller and more dense, they will shade the grass and kill it. But it will take five or more years before the little trees grow above the tall grass and another five years before they are tall and thick enough to shade the grass.

The grass's only chance to crowd out the new pines is in the first two or three years after the trees are planted. If the grass can shade the trees enough, soak up enough nutrients, and benefit from lack of rainfall, then the grass might win the competition. Grass and pine trees cannot live together; one must lose. Some of the trees had already died, about every tenth one.

Up the hill, where the soil was poorer and the grass more sparse, the trees were taller and already growing rapidly. These trees weren't competing with quack grass. They had sole rights to the nutrients, moisture, and sunlight.

Floyd and I noticed damage to the tops of many small trees. "Looks like snow did it," Floyd said. Many of the treetops were snapped off. A few trees were bent over at ground level and were turning up again with a crook about twelve inches from the base.

"Strange what heavy snow will do," Floyd said. "When these trees get bigger I think they'll still have crooks in their trunks, and people will wonder how the crooks got there. Only a few will remember the heavy snows of the '68–'69 winter and figure the snow deformed the trees."

Changing the subject, Floyd asked, "Say, what do you do with a woodchuck when it wants to crawl under your house?"

"I have no idea."

"He's been snoopin' around my porch for two or three days now, right in broad daylight too. I went for the shotgun yesterday when I saw it amblin' across my lawn, but when I got the gun it was gone. It's too bad Morty Oliphant isn't still around. He'd know what to do. Do you remember Morty?"

"Sure do, remember when I was a kid he would always bring his pet raccoon along with him to Wild Rose. Coon would sit on his shoulders."

Morty Oliphant was an old bachelor who had lived in a shack on the next farm south of Roshara. One of those gifted individuals who can talk with wild animals, Morty always had several living with him. But he moved to Wautoma before we acquired Roshara.

"Morty had a pet badger," Floyd said. "Lived under the floor in his house. The badger would come up into the house through a hole in the floor and eat. Badgers are vicious animals. I don't know how Morty tamed it, but he did.

"Course Morty was always talkin' to squirrels and chipmunks that lived around his house. I remember one time I was at his place—his pet coon was curled up on the bed. 'How's Snippy doin' today?' I asked Morty.

"Well, Morty called to the coon and it crawled down from the bed and ambled over to Morty's chair. 'How ya feelin' today, Snippy?' Morty said to the coon. That fat little raccoon cocked his head a little and looked right into Morty's eyes—they were talkin' together, that coon and Morty. And it wasn't just with sounds either. A lotta their talk can't be explained—sorta mysterious how feelin's of wild animals can be communicated to a human by them just sorta lookin' and makin' faces at each other.

"Morty could talk to animals like nobody else I ever knew. He would've taken my woodchuck home for a pet. Which reminds me, I'd better get home. The 'chuck is probably under the porch by now; maybe he's even in my kitchen."

"Don't you talk to the woodchuck like Morty does?" I asked.

"Nope, but I can sure battle him for what's left of the grub!"

XVI

Ole

At 8:30 Monday morning Ole Knutson parked his car in the shade of the end willow, near the tent.

"Let's get to work—sure is a fine day. Let's see, today we put up the beam. See you found one. Know how to put it up?" Ole asked.

"Afraid not—in fact, I don't have any idea."

My father came that morning to help with the beam, which was too heavy for Ole and me to handle.

Ole measured the length of the building again, then marked the beam. "Here's where you saw, and saw straight or we'll have troubles." He passed me the crosscut hand-saw. I tackled the job, but my flabby-muscled arm soon tired as I pushed and pulled the saw across the hard oak timber.

"You're kind of soft, ain't ya?" Ole said. "But you'll toughen up before we're through with this job. Here, let me have the saw for a minute."

Earlier Ole said he couldn't work anymore, that his arthritis bothered him too much, but he was handier with the handsaw than I'll ever be. His arm didn't tire, and soon the beam was the right length. A pile of sweet-smelling sawdust gathered on the ground under the beam; its aroma was a fringe benefit for an amateur carpenter who, despite ineptitude, enjoyed the smell of freshly cut old wood.

We grunted the beam into the granary. "Lucky aces, it fits," Ole said. "Lucky aces" turned out to be a phrase he often used. He also accompanied his work with song at times, usually something like "I Wonder Who's Kissing Her Now."

"Ladies and gentlemen, we now need a post to hold up the beam," Ole said.

I found another four-by-four beam and, with some pain, sawed it to make a post. Then we raised the beam into place, fastened it temporarily on one end, and slid the post under it. We put the hydraulic jack under the beam and raised it a half-inch before sliding the post into place.

"This'll make a good, tight fit, take the sag out of the upstairs floor too," Ole said.

We nailed the beam into place at the ends, and we were ready for the next project.

"Time for a rest, no sense hurryin', you know, live a lot longer if you don't. Do a lot better job too. Hurryin' makes for mistakes, and mistakes make for crooked buildings."

We measured the new door we had planned to go through the wall into the old chicken house. Then it was lunch time. Ole joined us under our canvas kitchen canopy near the tent. "Never eat much for lunch," Ole said. "Eat a good breakfast though—bacon and eggs, a bowl of fruit, toast. Sets me up for the whole day."

After lunch, Ole got out tobacco and cigarette paper and rolled a cigarette. The children had never seen anyone do that before. Carefully, Ole shook some tobacco onto the thin paper that he carefully held with one hand. Then he rolled the paper around the tobacco, wet one edge to seal it, and gave both ends a twist to hold the tobacco in.

"Country sure has changed around here since I was a kid. You know, I grew up only a little way from here. Came over from Norway when I was six, and my folks started me at the Chain O' Lake School. Had a terrible time; didn't know a word of English and here I was in school and supposed to be learnin' something. I learned English in a hurry. Had to.

"By the time I was thirteen I had to go to work. Started workin' for a carpenter, and I've been in the carpentry business ever since. Spent a lot of years in Chicago; lots of work for a carpenter there. Lots of things happenin' too. I remember prohibition, pretty dry time in Chicago, some said. But I had me a few anyway.

"Couple of neighbors and I got together and made a

batch of beer. Chipped in and bought the malt, mixed up the stuff, and bottled it. Put the bottles in my attic to cure. One night a few weeks later the wife and I were in bed when we was jarred by a loud explosion. Guessed it might be the beer that had blowed, so I went up to the attic. Sure enough, bottles blew up, glass all over the floor.

"I brought one of the bottles down to the bathroom and held it over the tub while I opened it. Come outta there like a fire hose. Bowled me over. Stuff was no good. Never made it again. Drunk others.

"Course, didn't have to make your own beer in Chicago during Prohibition. Al Capone and them fellers had places all over town. Cops'd walk right past the speakeasies, swingin' their sticks and laughin' while the beer trucks were unloadin'. Capone or somebody bought off the cops."

Then the conversation got around to fishing. I told Ole about some of our minor adventures at the pond.

"Talkin' about fishin'," Ole said, "reminds me of my brother-in-law Charlie. Always liked to go to Canada fishin'—never good enough around here. One time, though, Charlie wished he hadn't gone so far for his fish. Was out in a boat with a relative of his, a very plump girl. Everything was goin' well, except the fish weren't bitin'. Charlie, he tried to start the boat motor so's they could move to another place and suddenly the motor caught on fire. The girl, seein' the fire, jumped into the lake, leavin' Charlie to fight fire alone. He finally got the fire out, but not before he'd burned his hands and one leg. The girl couldn't get back in the boat so Charlie had to row a half-mile to shore with the girl hangin' on the back of the boat. Was agony, for his hands was severely burned, and the gal takin' it easy on the back made rowin' real difficult. Charlie laid in a Canadian hospital for a long time, not expected to live. Course the girl had no ill effects, thought it was a lark. Dunkin' didn't hurt her none."

After lunch we worked on the door frame and cut the hole through the wall. "That's all we can do now," Ole said. "We'll have to wait 'til you get the floor in before we can finish it off. I'll come back tomorrow, and we'll work on the new stairway."

I had bought a folding stairway from the lumberyard, the type used as a home attic ladder, as Ole had suggested. We could fold the ladder out of the way when not in use and have more room downstairs.

I patched the hole in the concrete floor with some quick cement, and then we all went swimming over at Silver Lake while we waited for the cement to harden.

While Ole and I were working on the cabin, the children had made friends with a gopher. The gopher was reddish brown with thirteen whitish stripes running down its back and sides; some of the stripes were broken into rows of whitish spots. It came up to the table and ate bread crusts the children threw to it, giving them an excellent excuse not to eat their crusts.

"Gotta save'm for the gopher," Jeff remarked. "He's a hungry little guy. Likes jelly crusts best."

When we returned from swimming, I saw the gopher running from under the tent. This was being too friendly, I thought, looking in the tent, but no damage was apparent. Only later did I learn why he had been there. We had pitched the tent over one of the gopher's entrance tunnels, and it had to crawl under the tent to get in. The gopher had no interest in the tent; he was only trying to get home.

Another incident had us mystified at first. After a swim one afternoon, we hung our wet bathing suits on a rope we had strung between two old fence posts near the drive. The next time Ruthie went for her suit, it was riddled with small holes. The holes were large enough to make the suit embarrassing, yet small enough to be repaired. The bathing suit was new and the only one on the line so affected.

A little detective work gave us the answer to the riddled suit. Many crickets lived in the tall grass under the rope, and for some reason they liked the taste of Ruthie's new suit. After that we hung the suit in a different place to dry.

The same evening we decided to remove some rotting wood that had been piled for years near the granary. The children and I were using Grandpa's pickup to haul the wood to a gully where it could finish rotting out of sight. Already many of the boards crumbled into pieces when we lifted them; soon they would disintegrate completely and return to the soil in the gully.

After loading the boards we came to several partially rotted blocks of firewood, overgrown with grass and difficult to remove. I gave one large block a kick with my boot to loosen it, and bumblebees swarmed from under it.

"Run!" I yelled, and we scattered in four directions. No one was stung, but we had ruined the bumblebee nest. Eggs and larvae were scattered on the ground and many angry bees flew around the disrupted nest. I got up enough courage to crawl into the truck and, with the windows tightly closed, drove the load of old wood to the gully.

As we threw the rotting boards, we disturbed another bumblebee nest. Again we ran. Finally we unloaded the rubbish in the dark, hoping the bees couldn't find us. No one was stung.

The next morning, every time we went near the bumblebee nest an angry bee chased us away. We weren't so lucky a few days later when picking up another pile of wood. It was a small woodpile, a few sticks Weston Coombes had forgotten. Jeff was gathering them up when he uncovered another bees' nest. I didn't know what had happened until I heard Jeff screaming and saw him running from the woodpile. Bumblebees were swarming all over him, stinging him furiously about the head and arms. I ran to him and beat the bees with my hat. I got stung only once.

When I got Jeff far enough away from the nest so the bees were no longer following, I looked at his stings, three huge welts on his neck and another on his arm. Jeff was frightened, but he was mad too. "I hate those bees, Dad. I hate 'em," was all he could say.

Under the willows, Jeff and I talked about how bumblebees pollinate flowers and clover and are an important part of nature. Nevertheless, Jeff could see no reason why bumblebees should be on this earth.

That evening Jeff complained of stomach cramps and developed a fever. The stings were having their effect. He vomited many times and then went to sleep. The following morning he had recovered, but he wouldn't go near the woodpile anymore that summer.

I suppose I relate this bumblebee episode because it was one of the times, and there were really quite few, when we were made aware that our attempt to renew and repair could be painful. We never really intended to disturb nature, only to clean up the rubble and mess that humans invariably leave.

Probably it was good that Jeff and I were stung. The sting of a bumblebee is uniquely devastating, but Jeff had learned the hard way that, even though the bees serve a vital purpose, nature can strike and strike hard. It was difficult to relate this to him, and, when I felt the huge swelling above my right eye, it was difficult to convince myself that I had had an elevating experience. The relationship of people to nature is not always easy to appreciate.

I knew, however, that Jeff and I might find some sort of mutual comfort in recounting our great bee episode—and that doubtless the story would get taller and taller through the years.

XVII

Deeper Feelings

When Ole came back the next morning, we worked on the folding stairway.

"Let's put the stairway close to the wall," Ole suggested. "Won't take up so much room when it's down, and when you snap it up, won't take any room at all."

We worked all morning cutting the hole in the upstairs floor and fitting the stairway in place. "Looks good," Ole said when we finished. "Now let's see if she works." He pulled on the rope to lower the stairway and it stuck against the cabin wall about halfway to the floor.

"Ladies and gentlemen," Ole said. "Looks like we done something wrong." He unfolded his measuring rule and checked the dimensions.

"Nothin' wrong with the measurements." He scratched his head, then sighted down the wall.

"Should have known," he said. "Granary leans a little bit to the northeast, just enough so the stairway won't work. Should have thought of that, just about every building leans a little, caused by the storms that come out of the southwest. Not a serious lean, but you gotta remember it when you put in the downstairs windows." Each time he moved the stairway up and down, it stuck in the same place against the wall.

"I'll come back tomorrow, and we'll move the stairway out a little, then it'll work. Why don't you start insulating the upstairs. Come on, I'll show you how to do it."

Ole showed me how to tuck the insulation between the rafters and staple it in place.

"Once you catch on to it you won't have any trouble. Get your wife to help you hold it."

When I carried the insulation upstairs I saw what looked like mouse droppings on the floor near the west window. We had seen the same thing shortly after we scrubbed the upstairs, and Ruthie had said, "If that's a mouse, you'd better get rid of it. You know what I think of mice. You'll not catch me sleeping up here if there're mice around."

It seemed unusual that a mouse would make its home upstairs in the cabin, for there were no nesting materials and nothing to eat. Promising Ruthie that I'd get rid of the mice, I had merely swept up the droppings and forgot the incident. But here was the evidence again, and in the same place on the floor. If it was a mouse, where was it staying?

Ruthie was finishing the lunch dishes. A good thing she wasn't upstairs. I was fitting the insulation between the rafters near the west window when I solved the mouse mystery.

A full-grown brown bat with a furry body and black skinlike wings flew out of its roosting place just before I covered it with insulation. Around the upstairs of the cabin the bat flew as I dodged to keep out of the way. Finally it landed on another rafter, and I crawled down from the upstairs to catch my breath and do some planning and thinking.

Why was I so surprised to find a bat in the upstairs, I asked myself. The old building was a likely place for a bat's home. No doubt it had lived upstairs in the granary for a long time—may even have been born there.

In a sense the bat was a part of Roshara, like the barn swallows and wrens and rabbits and deer. My first reaction to the bat was to get a club and kill it, get it out of our bedroom forever. I wanted to control, to prove that I was dominant.

Then as I thought about the bat and my relationship to it, I knew I must learn to understand and accept the bat for what it was, another animal with as much right to life as I. I decided not to harm the bat, but to get it out of the granary so it could find another place to live. We did want to reclaim the building for human use; in a sense, the bat had been a squatter. Taking a small stick back upstairs with me, I searched the rafters—no bat. Had it already gotten out? Was the problem solved?

In a roof board near the rafter where the bat landed, I noticed a hole and gently poked the stick inside. With several loud squeaks, the bat zoomed out and again circled the upstairs. As I skipped around trying to keep out of its way, uncomfortable thoughts raced through my mind. Was the bat angry enough to bite me? What about all the talk of rabies? Some say bats that appear otherwise normal may carry rabies. I wasn't looking forward to the series of painful shots.

Finally, the bat found a hole in the siding and escaped to the outside. I promptly plugged the escape hole and every other hole in the upstairs that looked large enough for a bat to enter. But the space from the top of the siding to the roof boards was still open, except for the insulation I pushed into it. I was hoping the bat would find a new home in the pump house; I wouldn't mind its living there.

Ruthie wasn't happy to learn there'd been a bat in our bedroom, but I said, "It's out now and I've plugged all the entrance holes." She only replied, "Get rid of the bat. I won't sleep there unless you do."

The next morning Ole and I redid the stairway and started work on the downstairs windows. I was sawing along the ceiling for a window opening when Ole said, "You know, it's a good thing you're a professor."

"Why's that?"

"You'll never make a carpenter; look how crooked that hole is you just sawed."

Ole was a perfectionist. To him it wasn't enough to measure closely; you measured exactly. You never said "it's about right"; it was either right, or it was wrong.

That evening Ruthie and I talked about carpenters and what it takes to be a good one. "It seems to me," I said, "that a carpenter is made up of about one-half a person who can measure and figure, one-quarter a person with the skill to handle a saw or hammer, and one-quarter a person with enough brawn and physical stamina to do the hard work."

"You missed one part of the person," Ruthie said. "A carpenter like Ole has to have a liberal portion of patience to put up with a would-be carpenter like you."

Anyhow, Ole was willing to continue to coach me as I blundered through sawing window openings, putting in insulation, and the like—and he seemed to enjoy it.

The following day we started cleaning out the chicken house attached to the west end of the granary; this was to become our porch. Unlike the granary, the chicken house had a dirt floor; after selling the chickens Weston Coombes had used the building for a woodshed. As the children, Ruthie, and I carried out many boxes of wood chips and pieces of stove wood, I thought of the Coombes family and how hard they had worked to cut the oak trees, haul them to the farmstead, and saw them into lengths for burning in their stoves.

The children complained of the dust, and I reminded them that Weston Coombes too must have had his nostrils full of the fine dirt from the wood and the dirt floor when he packed the oak sticks into the chicken house years before.

In one corner of the building, stuck under a two-by-four stud, was an old half-moon-shaped corn knife, its three-foot-long handle still straight and sound. As we examined the knife I told the kids of the cornfields that once grew at Roshara and were harvested each autumn.

John and Weston Coombes started cutting corn in late summer, before the killing frosts came to turn the green leaves brown. On those cool September mornings, the cows were milked early so the men could spend the day cutting and standing the cornstalks into shocks.

They dragged along a corn horse, a wooden device resembling a sawhorse with one set of legs. One end of the corn horse dragged on the ground. On the other end, near the legs, a metal rod was poked through a hole drilled in the center piece. John and Weston cut eight rows of corn in one direction, then eight rows across so that every shock had sixty-four hills of corn. Farmers in the area called this the eight-by-eight system.

The cornstalks were leaned against the corn horse, one-fourth of the stalks placed in each section made by the horse and the metal bar. When a corn shock was finished, Weston tied the top just below the tassels with binding twine.

Then he pulled out the metal pin and dragged the corn horse out from under the shock. Eight more hills down the field he and his father repeated the process. At day's end, shocks of corn, spaced exactly eight rows apart in both directions, marched up and down the field. Like plowing, it was the mark of a good farmer to make corn shocks exactly alike and line them up evenly and precisely.

Once the corn was shocked, Weston and John dressed warmly and went from shock to shock husking the ears and throwing them into piles to dry. Two or three days later they came by with their high-wheeled wagon, picked up the ears, and hauled them to the corncrib near the barn. Later they hauled the cornstalks to the barn, where they fed them to the cattle and pushed the uneaten stalks under the cows for bedding.

It was often below freezing when they sat by the shocks, day after day, peeling back the white husks and throwing the ears into piles. Sometimes they didn't finish before first snow and then the job was even more uncomfortable. But it had to be done as the cattle and pigs depended on the corn to get them through the long winter.

The Coombes family depended on the land for their existence; they respected it and knew it well. They accepted the crops the land gave them, never complaining of the hardships they experienced while working the soil.

As we talked about the Coombes family and their relationship to the land, I thought of what my family was gaining from the experience of reliving some of the past.

Without giving us food, Roshara offers much more than bread and milk. It gives my family a feeling of the great contribution a piece of land makes toward appreciating and understanding our environment. We are gaining insights into the hardships and pleasures of previous owners as we too experience the good, and the problems and challenges. We are growing in inner strength and purpose as we come to feel closer to the great heritage the land provides.

XVIII

Brotherhood with Life

The following Monday morning Ole and I fitted the windows into the upstairs. Finally a bedroom. That night, for the first time since we started remodeling the granary, we could sleep there.

From my mother we got an old metal bed that we shoved upstairs through the new stairway hole (after taking apart the stairway for the operation). Ruthie and I would have luxury, a bed with a mattress. Until this time we had slept on the ground in the tent, with air mattresses that never held air all night. But now we had a solid roof over our heads and a real bed. We had reached a major milestone.

We laid the canvas kitchen tarp on the floor and arranged the children's sleeping bags on it. We tucked the children into their sleeping bags, and a short time later Ruthie and I went to bed. There was no sign of the bat. I was a little worried because I thought Ruthie was worried, although she hadn't said a word. Somehow, I couldn't go to sleep, perhaps because the bed was too soft or the upstairs so roomy compared with the tent. Or maybe I was hearing wings.

A cool breeze blew the length of the upstairs. It was ideal for sleeping, but I couldn't sleep. Then I did hear something scratching. Scratch, scratch, then quiet. Then scratch, scratch again.

Maybe it's a tree limb rubbing against the roof, I thought.

Can't be a tree limb, none hangs over the roof. Maybe a bird? Unlikely. The wind? Only a little breeze tonight.

It was none of these things. I suddenly realized that the bat I had evicted last week was trying to get back into the upstairs. It was scratching along the bottom of the roof, looking for an opening. I remembered that the spaces between the siding and the roof boards were still open except for the insulation I'd pushed into them.

I hoped Ruthie wouldn't hear it and wake up. She'd have a fit.

I shined the flashlight along the rafters. Nothing. I listened again.

Then Ruthie, her blond hair mussed, turned toward me and said, "Why're you shining the light?"

"I thought you were asleep," I said nervously.

"I've been lying here thinking about Roshara and this old granary," she said.

"I'm afraid our visitor is back."

"You still worried about the bat?" she said quietly. "Here, I'll hold the flashlight and we'll look for it together. No sense worrying about a little bat; doubt it'd bother us anyway."

"But I thought you were the one who detested bats."

"Guess I'm changing my mind, Jerry, changing it about a lot of things since we've been coming to Roshara. Was thinking this afternoon, bats have to live too, you know."

I was too amazed to reply.

Together we carefully searched along the rafters and the insulation material. No bat. It must have given up and gone looking for some other roosting place.

The next morning I carefully fitted pieces of wood in each of the openings where the siding didn't quite come up to the roof. Now it was impossible for the bat to get in.

As I fastened the boards, I thought of how Ruthie and the children had changed, and yes, I had too, since acquiring Roshara. We've come closer together as a family to face the problems and glories of living. I felt a good glow of tenderness for everything and everybody—and especially for the old farm that did it.

At Roshara we move more slowly and deliberately, more thoughtfully without schedules dictating our activities.

While growing up on a farm, Ruthie always envied her cousins who lived in the city. She felt that farm girls were missing much of life, but now she knows how important the relationship of land is to life, as she welcomes each trip to Roshara.

The children have learned to play with one another as friends. They have also learned to play with the natural things in the outdoors—the old end willow, the friendly gopher. They collect stones, look for wildflowers, chase butterflies, and go fishing in the pond.

And I too have changed, although someone else could notice the transformation probably better than I.

During much of my life I've thought of the environment as something to be controlled, to be beaten down and defeated, utilized for essentially selfish, material purposes, to become something I wanted it to become. Slowly, I've come to realize that I'm only one of many creatures who must learn to live in concert with nature and all its living forms.

Everything I do at Roshara affects some part of its environment. I've come to realize how thoughtless I've been at times, how selfish to think that the environment and the land is only for people to use. As I realize that I am not especially special, but only one of many living things on this earth, my life becomes more rich and meaningful. I am at peace for I am part of a brotherhood with all that lives.

———

In that last week of our vacation we completed enough of the cabin so we could live inside. On the last day before returning to Madison, all that was left was to hang the cabin door.

I got up at sunrise and sat in the doorway of the cabin watching the sun send reddish-yellow rays through a bank of gray-black clouds. A wren chattered from the maple tree in the windbreak, then flew to another perch, then another, and finally landed on the roof of the wren house. Then it slipped into the house and was quiet.

Far down the dirt road that runs past the cabin, a cardinal whistled. It was unusual to hear the beautiful red bird this time of year; he was in his best singing form in the early spring.

A pair of barn swallows flew past, picking insects from the air with graceful sweeps.

A cloud of steam rose from the pond . . . cool morning air striking warm water. The steam cloud's eerie fingers stretched skyward, until they were evaporated by the sun that again warmed the air.

At a strange noise from the sky I looked up; four mallards flew over, one quacking loudly. They circled overhead and then turned toward the pond. They had probably been baby ducks on one of the neighboring ponds; we hadn't seen any on ours.

The children's gopher friend came out from under

the rock pile that was his home and sauntered toward me. He peered at me but wasn't at all bothered I was there. He was a friend.

A two-thirds-grown rabbit poked his head out from under a pile of boards no more than three feet away. He watched me, and I sat absolutely still, not moving for fear of frightening him. He nibbled grass at my feet, not concerned.

In the distance a farm dog barked; cattle were being driven to the barn for milking. I was reminded of my boyhood on the farm, the dewy mornings when our collie and I searched for the milk cows in the pasture farthest from the barn.

I thought again of John Coombes getting his Guernsey cows from the night pasture near the pond, his dog barking at the cows' heels as they came up the hill to the barn.

"Whatcha doin', Dad?" Jeff asked as he came out the cabin door, rubbing sleep from his eyes with one hand.

"Looking at the morning, Jeff, looking at the morning."

"Can I look too?"

I took Jeff in the crook of my arm.

We both watched the sun as it slowly climbed above Floyd's house and warmed us.

XIX

A New Life

This story has no end, only a stopping place. Our experiences at Roshara have been rich. But they are only an introduction to what we expect as the children grow older and explore more widely Roshara's treasures, and as Ruthie and I learn to know this deserted farm better.

We want to see the changes that occur at Roshara, as they surely will. We hope to see the passing of the seasons, so dramatic and exciting. We are eager to watch the pond as its level goes up and down with alterations in the water table.

We desire to find wildflowers we haven't seen before, and wild animals and songbirds not yet identified.

We want to watch the end willow that is growing old and dying. Each year more of its branches are claimed by the storms. And as the sunlight is allowed to filter to the ground under the willow, new plants start. Little oaks grow in the windbreak, as does a maple tree accidentally seeded by some animal or bird.

So this story is the beginning of an adventure, the beginning of our family's acquaintance with the outdoors and nature. It is a beginning wherein all five of us appreciate a life that is more than pay checks and neon lights.

As Roshara changes, the people change too. All grow older, and some die. Floyd Jeffers, our neighbor across the road, passed away before this book was finished. He was one of the old-timers. Floyd remembered when Roshara's hills grew potatoes and corn. He remembered when John Coombes planted the willow windbreak to keep the winter winds from the buildings.

Floyd loved the outdoors and was always learning more about it. The last summer he was alive he brought over to Roshara a pail filled with many kinds of wildflowers he couldn't identify. I stopped work on the cabin, and we sat in the shade of the willows with my wildflower book, keying out the names of the flowers.

He fed the birds at his feeder the year around. Chickadees sat on his hand as he fed them, squirrels ate corn at his feet.

But now Floyd is gone, a link to the past that is departed, not too unlike the end willow that is showing its age and may soon be blown over by a windstorm and killed.

So Roshara changes. The old pass away and the young, like my three children, take over and carry on.

This story, like the cabin, will never be finished. We hope to add to it each year as we accumulate new experiences.

Our cabin will always be primitive. We want it that way. When we come to Roshara we are searching for a different life from what we know in the city. We will heat the cabin with a wood-burning stove; we'll have no running water or electricity for the next few years, maybe never, and no telephone.

We come to Roshara seeking quality in our lives. And we are finding it in the sunsets, the pond, the deer that run by the cabin, the rainstorms that pound the cabin roof, the bluebirds that nest in the hollow fence posts.

We are finding a new life in the fresh air we breathe, untainted by coal smoke and automobile exhaust. We are finding it in the peaceful, flower-covered hills we explore.

We are finding quality in our lives by watching Roshara change according to nature's plan, not according to our plan.

We want to see the wildflowers growing undisturbed in the oak wood lots. We want to watch the little black oak trees grow.

We don't want to make over or tamper with what is taking place. We only want to be there to see what's happening. We are observers of God's great plan, and we are thankful for the opportunity to see, and hear, and feel, and smell the magnificence of it all.

EPILOGUE

Fifty years ago I began this book by writing about an old black willow tree. At that time the tree was already nearly sixty years old. It was surely not a tree you would call beautiful, as you might imagine describing a sugar maple or a balsam fir. But what it lacked in beauty it made up for in resilience, for that old black willow, now approaching 110 years old, still stands at the end of the windbreak. Not that it hasn't suffered; it's been struck by lightning more than once, and two years ago a wicked windstorm nearly demolished it—or so I thought. But the willow still lives, continuing to contribute to the work of the windbreak that protects our cabin and outbuildings from the fiercest winds out of the west.

Roshara has seen many changes since this book was originally published. When we bought this land, my brothers and I divided the original one hundred acres equally, thirty-three and a third acres each. In 1993, I bought my brother Darrel's share of the farm. And in 2011, I purchased an additional sixty acres from my neighbor to the north, land that is part of the original 160 acres that Thomas Stewart homesteaded in 1867. Hardwoods, black oak, bur oak and white oak, white birch, and black cherry grow on these acres, which have never been farmed. Most of these sixty acres are studded with enormous boulders left behind by the glacier that began receding from this landscape ten thousand years ago.

Over time we have watched what was once a six-acre cornfield turn itself into a beautiful stand of self-seeded white pine trees. The old white pine windbreak that the Coombes family planted to prevent the soil from blowing away in the drought years of the 1930s now stands straight and tall and provides the seed stock for several thousand white pines.

Every year that we have owned Roshara, we have planted trees here, mostly red pines, but some Norway spruce and jack pines as well. Some years we planted a couple hundred trees; one year we planted more than seven thousand. Much of our land is now tree covered, and some of the first trees we planted are now more than fifty feet tall.

Roshara includes the original pond I wrote about in 1969, plus part of a second one. These water-table ponds, which rise and fall as the aquifer rises and falls, provide nesting grounds for mallards and wood ducks, Canada geese, sandhill cranes, and a host of other water-loving birds, plus frogs, turtles, and other creatures.

We began restoring the prairie, about eight acres, in the mid-1970s. It now flourishes with native wildflowers and grasses, bluebirds, honeybees and bumblebees, tree swallows, and other species that enjoy an expanse of sun-swept open land. The changes in Roshara's prairie are fascinating and continual; thirty years into it I still spot flowers and grasses I haven't seen here before.

A wild lupine patch that was less than a quarter-acre in size when we purchased the land has grown to several acres, with little effort on our part other than removing nearby self-seeded Scotch pines that were competing for sun. And while I didn't know anything about Karner blue butterflies back in 1966, I certainly know about them now, as our lupine patch is home to several hundred of these federally protected little beauties.

The cabin, built as a granary in 1912, continues to provide shelter for our family. We've made several additions, and what began as one room with a low-ceilinged loft now has four additional rooms—and indoor plumbing, which we installed in 1992.

Just as the land and the buildings at Roshara have changed and grown, so has our family. In 1966 our children were four, three, and two years old. They grew up hiking Roshara's trails, climbing its trees, digging in its dirt. Today, Sue is a second-grade teacher in the Madison school district and a published author. Steve has worked for more than thirty years as a photojournalist, the past twenty for the *Wisconsin State Journal* in Madison. Jeff is an investment counselor in Avon, Colorado.

Sue's two boys, Josh and Ben, who grew up in Madison, have spent many hours at the farm. Jeff's three kids, Christian, Nicholas, and Elizabeth, spend time every year at Roshara as well. We all share a love of the many trails that thread past the ponds and through deep woods, across the open prairie, up the steep hills, and along the long valleys. But what has tied the family together most indelibly at Roshara is our vegetable garden. Over the years the garden—at one time more than an acre in size—has been a subtle yet powerful source of nature education for the kids and grandkids. Gardening's annual cycle of tilling, planting, tending, and harvesting has kept our family close to the earth while teaching the children that all life depends on clean air, water, and soil. Today our garden is less than a quarter-acre in size, yet it provides enough fresh vegetables for three families.

The title I chose for this book upon its publication in 1970 remains true today. The land still lives, and Roshara still lives. There is much to be learned from nature, no matter one's age. My hope is that these lessons will help us realize that the future of this country—indeed, the future of our world—depends upon an understanding and appreciation of nature in all its dimensions.

Jerry Apps
2019

PHOTO BY STEVE APPS

Jerry Apps was born and raised on a central Wisconsin farm. He is a former county extension agent and professor emeritus at the University of Wisconsin–Madison, where he taught for thirty years. Today he works as a rural historian, creative writing instructor, and full-time writer. He has created five documentaries with Wisconsin Public Television, has won several awards for his writing, and won a regional Emmy Award for the TV documentary *A Farm Winter*. He and his wife, Ruth, divide their time between their home in Madison and their farm, Roshara, in Waushara County.

Jerry is the author of more than forty fiction, nonfiction, and children's books on rural history, country life, and the environment. *The Land Still Lives* was his first.

Discover More Books
by Jerry Apps

Simple Things: Lessons from the Family Farm

Never Curse the Rain: A Farm Boy's Reflections on Water

Whispers and Shadows: A Naturalist's Memoir

The Quiet Season: Remembering Country Winters

*Roshara Journal: Chronicling Four Seasons,
Fifty Years, and 120 Acres*

Living a Country Year: Wit and Wisdom from the Good Old Days

Every Farm Tells a Story: A Tale of Farm Family Values

Garden Wisdom: Lessons Learned from 60 Years of Gardening

Old Farm County Cookbook: Recipes, Menus, and Memories
(with Susan Apps-Bodilly)

Old Farm: A History

Wisconsin Agriculture: A History